A CENTURY OF SPORTS CARS

A CENTURY OF SPORTS CARS

BROCKHAMPTON PRESS

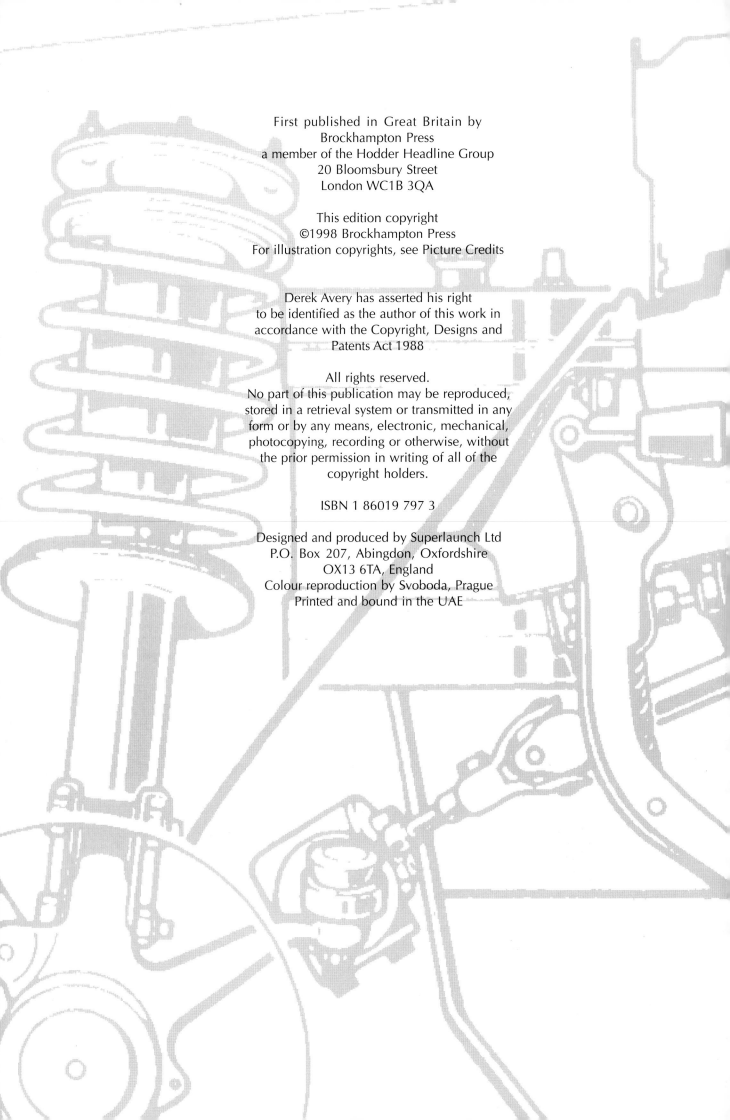

First published in Great Britain by
Brockhampton Press
a member of the Hodder Headline Group
20 Bloomsbury Street
London WC1B 3QA

ISBN 1 86019 797 3

Designed and produced by Superlaunch Ltd
P.O. Box 207, Abingdon, Oxfordshire
OX13 6TA, England
Colour reproduction by Svoboda, Prague
Printed and bound in the UAE

CONTENTS

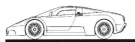

PUBLISHER'S NOTE

The body of this new volume *A Century of Sports Cars* is a survey of 100 cars from around the world, arranged chronologically, with the emphasis very definitely upon the second half of the twentieth century, that is, after the Second World War.

The definition of a sports car found in any dictionary will not necessarily accord with everyone's own ideas, and so within this compilation we have tried to abide by the manufacturers' own classifications. The book could not have been presented in its current form in this breadth and depth of scope without the help of the many manufacturers and enthusiasts who have been most generous in contributing information and pictures. Our deepest thanks go to them all, in the hope that they will continue to encourage the pursuit of our dreams.

The Benz patent Tricycle of 1886

Karl Benz (1844–1929) created his first engine in 1879, and patented the first automobile in Berlin on 29 January 1886

FOREWORD

The car industry was born with the Benz Tricycle; since then, the automobile has captured the dreams of every small boy and a great many grown men. Some have strived to achieve the ultimate sports car: a combination of the speed felt through every moving part of the vehicle with the beauty of its form, lavishly cared for and polished.

A century ago, there were only six cars on the roads of Britain. The first had not appeared here until the summer of 1895, when the Hon Evelyn Ellis shipped over his French-built Panhard, and drove it from the docks at Southampton to his home in Datchet.

The first British motor show, later that year, exhibited only five cars. The following year the very first British car was launched, the Daimler Phaeton, based on German patents. A century later, 220 exhibitors and as many models from 60 manufacturers packed the British International Motor Show.

GLOSSARY

chassis: the frame to which the body of a car is attached.

connecting rods: the con-rods and crankshaft are regarded as one assembly.

convertible: a car with a folding or removable roof, and side windows.

coupé: a closed, two-door car with two side windows.

crankshaft: the main shaft in an engine, joined to the pistons by the con-rods, which together convert the linear motion of the pistons into a rotary motion.

cubic capacity: the total capacity of an engine, expressed in terms of the volume swept by the pistons in the cylinders.

desmodromic: a mechanism in which the driving part is kept in constant contact with the part being driven, without any secondary return mechanism; for example a twin-cam arrangement that has no return spring.

engine configuration: *inline*, an engine which has its cylinders arranged one behind the other; *boxer* or *flat*, an engine in which the cylinders are horizontally opposed; *flat twin*, a horizontally-opposed 2-cylinder engine; or *Vee*, which is configured as two banks of 1, 2, 3, 4, 5, 6 or even 8 cylinders set at an angle to each other.

four wheel drive: a car in which all four wheels can transmit the power from the engine to the road, whether or not this facility is permanently engaged.

front wheel drive: a car having front wheels which transmit the power from the engine to the road, as distinct from rear or four-wheel drive.

fuel injection: a system of introducing atomised liquid fuel under pressure directly into the combustion chambers of an internal combustion engine.

hydropneumatic: a suspension or any other system that uses both liquid and gas.

Index or **performance index:** a classification index used at the Le Mans 24-Hour race to assess performance level related to factors such as fuel consumption.

long tail: a type of bodywork used for racing cars, the rear of which is highly streamlined; distinguished from short-tail designs, which have truncated rear styling seen for example on the Porsches at Le Mans.

monocoque: a car design without a separate chassis and body, in which all or most of the load is taken by the skin, without any need for additional loadbearing members.

multi-valve: an engine in which each cylinder has three or more valves.

open tourer (torpedo): a car with a folding or removable hood and a fixed windscreen.

ohc or **overhead camshaft:** a shaft having one or more cams attached to it, used to operate the inlet and exhaust valves in an engine. It is so described when it is situated on the upper part of the engine.

pre-selector gearbox: a system which enables the driver to chose in advance the required gear.

piston: a thick disc that is forced to move up and down within its cylinder by the expanding gases in the cylinder head.

port (two-stroke): openings along a cylinder that allow the air and fuel mixture to be fed into, and exhaust gases to escape from, a two-stroke or valveless engine.

rear-wheel drive: a car having rear wheels which transmit the power from the engine to the road, as distinct from front-wheel drive or four-wheel drive.

roadster: a two-seater car without side windows.

rotary engine: consists of the stator and a rotor in which the movements are cyclical, for example a Wankel engine.

saloon: a closed four-door car, with four side windows.

sleeve-valve engine: one in which sliding sleeves that alternately cover and uncover ports in a cylinder have been substituted for the standard valves.

straight-through gearbox: a mechanism which simplifies the gearbox by allowing the drive shaft to drive the propeller shaft directly for the most frequently used ratio.

stroke: the phases of a four-stroke engine are induction, compression, combustion and exhaust. In a two-stroke engine, the induction and compression phases form the first stroke, while the combustion and exhaust phases form the second stroke.

torque converter: a hydraulic device, used particularly in automatic gearboxes, for the gradual transmission of torque to the wheels.

track: the distance between the front or rear wheels, when measured from the centre of one tyre tread to the other; *see also* **wheelbase.**

transmission: denotes the series of mechanisms that transmit the rotary power of the engine to the drive of the wheels.

turbo or **turbocharger:** a form of supercharging in which a turbine driven by exhaust gases powers a centrifugal fan or blower.

two-door saloon: a closed two-door car with four side windows.

two-stroke: a simple type of internal combustion engine, often used to power motorcycles; *see also* **stroke.**

valves: most of the modern four-stroke piston engines employ overhead valves (ohv) which inlet the fuel charge and exhaust the spent gases. Overhead valves can be operated indirectly by pushrods and rockers actuated by a gear-driven camshaft in the engine block, or directly by overhead camshafts. High-performance engines usually have multi-valve cylinder heads and use one or more overhead camshafts, one to operate the inlet valves and the other to operate the exhaust valves. In this way, a twin-overhead camshaft V8 engine will have four camshafts, two for each bank of cylinders.

voiturette: an early two-seater open touring car.

volumetric supercharger: a device used to compress air drawn into the combustion chamber of an engine; unless stated to the contrary, the term refers to a volumetric compressor driven by the propeller shaft itself.

wheelbase: the distance between the front and rear wheels, measured from the centre of the wheels; *see also* **track**. A long wheelbase, narrow-track car would tend to be good in a straight line – for example, a drag racer – whereas a short wheelbase, wide track car would be better able to change direction.

INTRODUCTION

One hundred years ago, motoring was the preserve of gentlemen, and a leisure pastime that had somewhat raffish connotations. Much of the motorist's time was spent attending to mechanical breakdowns, and motoring was thus most certainly a sport, although at that time there was no such beast as a sports car. Up to the time of the First World War, the majority of so-called sporting cars were standard touring models,

The Paris-Madrid race of 1903 was never completed, being curtailed at Bordeaux after a memorable chain of tragedies. The day's racing accounted for a total of ten deaths with countless others, both drivers and spectators, being injured. Entrants amounted to 300 cars, of which 275 actually started, including twelve De Dietrichs, 14 Mors, 15 Panhards and four Renaults. Two of the latter were driven by Louis and Marcel Renault.

It was estimated that 100,000 Parisians had made their way to Versailles for the start of the race, which was scheduled to commence at 3.30am on 24 May. The cars departed at two-minute intervals, with the Englishman Charles Jarrott drawing the lot to be first away. However, so reckless had been the driving and the behaviour of the spectators that only 100 cars completed the first stage to Bordeaux.
Top: Louis Renault is told of his brother Marcel's fatal accident at Couhé-Vérac by his other brother, Fernand. The mechanic, who has heard nothing because of the noise of the engine, smiles unknowingly
Centre right: the Belgian driver Jenatzy, driving a 89.5kW (120hp) Mercedes, takes the Rochefort bend during the 1905 Gordon Bennett Cup. The race was held to the west of Clermont-Ferrand in France and was the sixth and last. It was won by the Frenchman Théry at an average speed of 77.7km/h (48.3mph)
Right: a pit-stop, 1908-style. Lautenschlager changes a wheel of his French Grand Prix-winning Mercedes

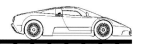

perhaps lighter and with a little more power and more austerely equipped, but with little to be commended technically.

The French motor industry was booming as the twentieth century neared. France was regarded as the spiritual home of the motor car and of motor racing, with such great marques as Delahaye, De Dietrich, De Dion and Peugeot leading the way. The French were also in the vanguard in the quest for speed. Motor racing meant French motor racing and for years the grand prix was to mean the French Grand Prix, with few foreign challengers to compete in that prestigious pursuit.

Camille Jenatzy's torpedo-shaped electric car broke through the 100km/h (62mph) barrier in 1899. In that same year manufacturers first began to realise not only that they could gain important publicity from their products' speed and reliability, but also that their designers were learning fast about suspensions, brakes, valves and pistons from their endeavours in competition. These events were invariably being run on roads which by today's standards were utterly appalling.

Some races were being organised for specific marques, the first of these being for Mors cars. City-to-city races also grew in popularity. The first of these to cross frontiers was the race from Paris to Amsterdam and back, a distance of 1,430km (889 miles). The first winner of this race was a Panhard, at an average speed of 43.3km/h (26.9mph).

As the twentieth century dawned, the first circuit race was run over two laps on the roads around Mélun, south-east of Paris. Within just a few years the die was cast for the manufacturers, who had even further opportunities to exhibit their wares and to test their skills as both the Targa Florio and the first national grand prix, the French, took place in 1906.

Top: *Ferdinand Porsche on his way to victory in the 1910 Prince Henry Trials*
Above centre: *Georges Boillot emerges from a bend in the 1913 French Grand Prix*
Left: *a Chénard-Walcker at Le Mans, 1929*

TARGA FLORIO

The oldest and only extant race to take place on open roads, this is also the second-oldest sports car race in the world, and our only link with those spectacular city to city races that were run at the turn of the nineteenth century.

The first race took place in 1906, a year after the Tourist Trophy (TT) event had been initiated by the Automobile Club and held on the Isle of Man. The Automobile Club soon gained royal patronage in 1907, to become the RAC. The Italian race was the brainchild of the wealthy enthusiast and successful racing driver Vincenzo Florio, and the course devised for it was a tortuous one that twisted and turned, rose and fell, from the coastal plains through the mountains and valleys of Sicily.

Drivers departed at timed intervals, and were required to drive flat-out over 31 laps of a 145km (90-mile) circuit that was excruciatingly demanding. There was certainly none more daunting, and in 1906 all the runners lacked sophistication; they were heavy, solid, generally unreliable and no great joy to drive at speed over rutted mule tracks round hairpin bends with a sheer drop on one side.

The first race managed to attract ten starters, of which six finished. Their biggest problem appears to have been the constant replacement of punctured tyres, most of the starters setting out with as many as eight spares. The winning average speed was an amazing 48km/h (30mph).

Every race was won by an Italian car in the years leading up to the First World War, and Florio spent a great deal of effort and money to attract a wider range of competitors, all to no avail. Things improved from 1919 onwards, with the shorter medium Madonie circuit of 108km (67 miles) being used, and four laps being run so that the total race distance covered remained the same and the spectators benefitted. The field was now swollen by French and British competitors driving a new breed of 2.5-litre (152cu in) race-bred Peugeots, Mercedes and dohc straight-eight Ballots pitted

Left: *Alfred Neubauer in his Austro-Daimler Sascha, No 46, poses before the start of the 1922 Targa Florio; circled is Ferdinand Porsche*

Below left: *the eventual winners, Stirling Moss and Peter Collins, during the chronometer-counted part of the 1955 race*

Bottom: *1970, with Kinnunen and Rodrigues taking the lead in their factory-entered lightweight 908/03 Porsche, to set a new lap record of 128.571km/h (79.907mph) in the final lap*

against the pre-war Fiats, Italas and Alfas. Part of the 1919 race was run in a snowstorm, and it was eventually won by Boillot in a Peugeot. He spun and crashed within metres of the finishing line, which he crossed triumphantly in reverse. He was then forced to drive back to the scene of the accident and drive back across the line bonnet-first, because his original 'win' was disputed by the officials.

Below: *the fiftieth race was the 1966 event, won by Müller and Mairesse driving a Porsche Carrera 6; it was also Porsche's sixth victory*

Bugatti reigned supreme between 1925 and 1929, and managed a second and third place in 1930, when Alfa Romeo took over the mantle which it was to bear until 1935. The race when the laurels passed from Bugatti to Alfa was one of the most spectacular Targa Florios, with the 2-litre (122cu in) grand prix Alfa driven by Achille Varzi coming under a constant onslaught from one Bugatti after another during its seven hours. Varzi had lost his spare wheel, and his petrol tank had been holed; furthermore, he had been delayed by a fire. The Bugatti chase was led by Divo until he crashed out, then by Chiron with such gusto that he was lucky to escape a violent death. He failed by less than two minutes to catch Varzi, whose average speed was 78km/h (48.5mph), far faster than that of any previous winner. Varzi left the Alfa team and for the following two years the race was won by Tazio Nuvolari.

The race was run over a short course of two laps around the 141.9km (88.2-mile) Favorita Park circuit in 1937, when the honours went to Maserati, which continued to win until 1940.

The event resumed in 1948 and ran for three years over a 977km (670-mile) Giro di Sicilia course, being dominated by Ferrari and Alfa with Cisitalia coming in second and third in 1948.

It reverted to the short Madonie circuit in 1951, when it also became a strictly sports-car event and was the first year in which cars had to comply with international sports-car regulations. It also provided the only win ever for a British manufacturer, the Cortese-driven Frazer Nash.

It became a qualifying event for the Sports Car Championship in 1958; this was the same year in which Vincenzo Florio, its founding father with a passion for cars, died.

The last race to count towards the Championship was run in 1973, the fifty-seventh Targa Florio. Conditions had improved beyond recognition from those that had prevailed back in 1906; the race was won by Gijs van Lennep and Herbert Müller in a Porsche RSR, at an average speed of 115.39km/h (71.27mph). The same combination came fourth in that year's Le Mans event.

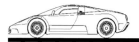

The long-distance races of the era included the Coupe Boillot, held at Boulogne; the Bol d'Or, a 24-hour race for cars and cycles of up to 1,100cc (67.1cu in) capacity, introduced in the year before that at Le Mans; and numerous *voiturette* events, as well as the *grands prix du tourisme*.

In the period immediately following the Armistice, France retained her pre-eminence through the marques of Bugatti, Delage and Ballot in grand prix racing, and through Delage and Talbot in the *voiturette* events. The new form of motor racing was provided by the advent of the Le Mans 24-Hour race, which was promoted by the French as the supreme test for their own cars; they did take nine of the first 12 placings during the first four years, through the marques of Chénard-Walcker and Lorraine-Dietrich.

This last was perhaps the best-known of the sports-car marques. The cars were big, rough and rugged, with 3.5-litre (213.6cu in) long-stroke 6-cylinder engines and twin carburettors, a high

compression ratio and dual ignition. In works-entered guise at Le Mans in 1924 they filled second and third places, in 1925 first and third, and in 1926 first, second and third, respectively.

Louis Delage produced the classic DI 2-litre (122cu in) in 1924. It was low-built, light and fast, with 4-wheel brakes as standard; a responsive car that represented to many sporting enthusiasts the quintessence of all the finest in French motoring. In the following year Delage unveiled the GL ohc 6-litre (366.1cu in) series. Although not successful at Le Mans, Delage did much better with his 2-litre (1.22cu in) and 1.5-litre (91.5cu in) racing cars, which swept the board in the grands prix between 1925 and 1927.

A 1926 Amilcar Type C0, left, alongside a Type CGS or Surbaissé. Both models are now exhibited at the Musée National de l'Automobile, Collection Schlumpf (National Automobile Museum), Mulhouse, France

The Anglo-French consortium of Sunbeam Talbot Darracq produced a wide range of cars under the guidance of Louis Coatalen. They included luxury, touring, sporting and racing models, but one of the most successful mid-1920s cars was the 12/32 Sport. Powered by a 1,600cc (97.6cu in) pushrod engine, it was easily capable of 100km/h (62mph), a speed which it reliably maintained mile after mile. By the end of the decade, Darracq had added yet more power and opted for a 6-cylinder unit.

Meanwhile, Gabriel Voisin was making his reputation for beautifully constructed machines that were both fast and luxurious, which he built throughout the decade. He toyed with Vee and inclined 12-cylinder engines, Cotal gearboxes, sleeve valves, and even a sun roof; although the latter was vacuum-operated and not introduced until 1926. He also built grand prix cars with aerofoil streamlined bodies, as early as 1923. He was a true innovator; in 1927, he produced a special with

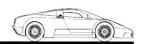

an inline 8-cylinder engine. This was a high-performance car, which achieved an excellent average speed of 181.8km/h (113mph) over a 24-hour period.

Two of the most successful French light cars of the time were the Amilcar and the Salmson models. For a decade these companies competed against each other for sales and sporting success. The Amilcar appeared first, arriving towards the end of 1920. Initially it was an economy car with no sporting pretensions, with its 904cc (55.1cu in) side-valve engine producing 13.4kW (18bhp). The company's first sporting model was the C4 of 1922, with a 1,044cc (63.7cu in) 17.1kW (23bhp) engine. Two of these were entered in the 1922 Bol d'Or, one of which won at an average speed of 64km/h (40mph). Amilcar continued to develop, and in 1926 produced the 4-cylinder CGS or Surbaissé model which had cycle-type wings. By then, the company employed 1,200 people and was turning out some 35 vehicles per day, mainly sporting models. Sadly the company ended in bankruptcy and disgrace, but left behind a legacy of potent light cars which were well able to surpass the 161km/h (100mph) mark, and a succession of three straight first-in-class wins in the Brooklands 200.

Salmson had begun insignificantly before the First World War, but in 1919 decided to replicate a 2-cylinder British GN under licence. Realising that this was potentially limiting, the company then switched to a 4-cylinder model in 1921. This new model had an 1,100cc (67cu in) engine set very far back in the frame, a two-seater body and no differential. The engine used a single pushrod per cylinder, which also acted as a pull rod for the inlet valve.

This interesting development was derived from Salmson's involvement with aero engines. Its maximum speed of about 80km/h (50mph) was not considered very fast, and so a twin-cam engine was developed to rectify this. This in turn was followed by a grand prix model, which took first and second places in the 1923 Bol d'Or albeit with especially light *papier maché* bodies. The company went on to produce supercharged cars with front-wheel brakes and cowled radiators. When

Amilcar introduced its twin-cam six, Salmson riposted with a 104kW (140bhp) straight-eight. However, here again decline set in towards the end of the decade, and by 1934 Salmson was again linked again with the British company.

Two of the models that were most advanced mechanically to appear in France at the start of the 1920s were the 2-litre Ballot, and the 6-cylinder Hispano-Suiza. Ballot was one of the most promising new marques to appear after the First World War. The company had made engines for a number of years, and eventually produced 3 and 5-litre (183 and 305cu in) racing cars which had been designed for it by the Peugeot engineer, Ernest Henry. Its 2-litre (122cu in) 2LS Sports model had a twin shaft-driven overhead camshaft and a 16-valve engine that developed 55.9kW (75bhp) at 4,000rpm. It was the most advanced sports car of its day, and possessed all that the sporting enthusiast could dream of in 1922, being capable of 148km/h (92mph). Ballot introduced the 2LTS in 1925. Its hemispherical combustion chambers and large valves gave the model the ability to cruise at 100km/h (62mph) for hours on end. It was joined by the first of the straight-eight RH cars in 1928, which remained in production until after the company's merger with Hispano-Suiza.

The big Hispanos were the work of Marc Birkigt. Each bore on its radiator cap a flying-stork statuette, the insignia of Guynemer's ace squadron of Hispano-engined SPAD fighters. Like the Ballot, these most beautifully proportioned machines possessed brakes to match their performance; they acted on all four wheels, were servo-assisted and had finned-aluminium drums.

André Dubonnet, better known as an apéritif entrepreneur, entered the Coupe Boillot privately in 1921 and won it, in his standard Hispano four-seater. This prompted Hispano to enter a works team in the following year, using a short-chassis version with larger 8-litre (488cu in), 8-cylinder engines and a 149kW (200bhp) output. Hispano won the Boulogne event again in 1922 and 1923, and as a result adopted the name Boulogne Hispano

for the model. One of these also won the Spanish Touring Car Grand Prix, again driven by Dubonnet, who also took seventh place in the Targa Florio in 1924. The Hispano-Suiza was in a class of its own, though the marque's sporting character began to decline after 1923 when the company ceased to support sports events; nonetheless, the short-wheelbase Boulogne had been a truly magnificent beast.

Of course, there were many other French marques that illuminated the 1920s, including those of such notable visionaries as Gabriel Voisin. His little garage in Versailles produced a low-built, front-wheel drive car, powered by a supercharged 1,100cc (67cu in) engine, with its gearbox forward and blower behind. It was all the work of the engineer and designer, Jean Grégoire.

Panhard and Peugeot also built sports cars during the decade. The Panhards were unusual in having sleeve-valve engines. Chénard-Walcker cars came first and second in the 1923 Le Mans 24-Hour race, also won the 1924 Circuit des Routes Pavées and recorded a fourth place in the 1925 Coupe Boillot with a 4-litre (244cu in) straight-eight.

The radiator, badge and the famous flying stork emblem of the Hispano-Suiza

LE MANS

During the early 1920s, car lights were either dim acetylene or dubious electricity. In consequence, the Le Mans 24-Hour race was conceived primarily as a night race, with the intention of bringing about improvements in the lighting systems of production cars.

The race was inaugurated by the efforts of Charles Faroux, and the then Secretary-General of the Automobile Club de l'Ouest, Charles Durand. It was to prove also to be a test of the endurance of the entire vehicle in this round-the-clock race. Grand prix events were already being held on the circuit of roads south of the city of Le Mans and so this became the obvious location, although the road surface was quite appalling. Some parts resembled narrow farm tracks with only a rutted natural surface, a few were tarmacadamed, and yet others again were cobbled. Furthermore, representations had to be made to the government to close the highways for such a long period. However, the event did take place, beginning in 1923 with 35 starters.

The rules stipulated that cars with full

four-seater bodywork could compete only if the ballast equivalent of three passengers was carried; the smallest cars were exempt from this rule, however. A certain number of laps had to be run with the car's hood up, and the driver was required to carry out all refuelling and repairs himself, tools for the purpose being carried in the car. The first 322km (200 miles) had to be completed without anything being

Above: *1951 at Le Mans, and Porsche makes its first appearance in the event that it would come to dominate in later years. Car number 46 is a 356/2 type (Gründ coupé) that won its 1,100cc class, driven by Veuillet and Mouche*
Below: *a Jaguar D-Type, three-times winner at Le Mans in 1955, 1956 and 1967, and the emblem of the marque's racing career*

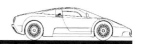

Above: *the start of the 1966 race which ended incredibly, 24 hours later, in a photo-finish*

done to the car by way of repair or refuelling. The lap distance was 17.3km (10.73 miles), and the first race, which was completed by no fewer than 30 of the 35, was won by Lagache and Leonard in a Chénard-Walcker at an average speed of 92km/h (57.2mph). This marque also provided the second-place winner, ahead of the more famous names such as Bugatti, Delage, Salmson, Amilcar and Peugeot.

From its inception in these early amateurish experimental years, the Le Mans 24-Hours was held in a party atmosphere, with fireworks displays, moving picture shows, concerts that were transmitted by radio from the Eiffel Tower, jazz bands and even an orchestra. The pits were brilliantly illuminated so that the spectators saw all the action, and the drivers could devour plates of chicken, hot soup and the odd bottle of Champagne. The night driving was made easier by a circuit of army searchlights, mounted on Renault trucks, which lit up the bends at

Mulsanne, Arnage and Pontlieu in addition to supplying some sort of pathway on the straights.

The event was an instant success; in 1925 it had already expanded to 49 starters, including the first US entrant in a Model 70 6-cylinder Chrysler, and a grandstand built by the Automobile Club de l'Ouest stood opposite the pits. It was also in 1925 that for the first time a 'Le Mans' start was used, and the event has never looked back.

Below: *a Type 962C carried the Porsche flag at the 1988 race*

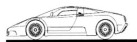

However, at the end of the 1920s, motoring was still largely the preserve of the moneyed and leisured. As their attention turned to sports motoring, they became the proud owners of powerful sports models developed purely for the pleasure of driving fast on open roads. This élite demanded large engines, which were often fitted with superchargers for that extra boost of impressive power. The fast touring car had become the sports car, and ushered in one of the most exciting eras in motoring history. Many cars could now top the psychologically significant 161km/h (100mph) mark, and as manufacturers began to exploit the publicity that they gained through racing success, marques such as Alfa Romeo, Bugatti, Bentley, Chevrolet and Duesenberg all gained their reputations on the racetracks during the 1930s.

However, for the majority of people the best sports cars between 1919 and 1939 came from Bugatti, which made high-performance cars in all sizes. Ettore Bugatti built a team of modified

Type 13 cars in 1914, but hostilities forced him to close his factory at Molsheim, France, before he had the opportunity of testing them. However, he managed to secrete three of them at Molsheim and a further two which he took with him to Le Mans. After the First World War, he was able to enter three of these cars in the *voiturette* grand prix at Le Mans, where one of them triumphed. Bugatti continued production of these small Type 13s with their 4-cylinder 1,368cc (83.5cu in) engines. Longer wheelbase models were designated Type 22s. The Type 23, which appeared in 1920 with a roller-bearing crankshaft and an engine capacity of 1,453cc, took the first four places in the 1921 Italian *voiturette* grand prix at Brescia. This resulted in the car becoming popularly known by the place name, and later led to all

A 1927 Bugatti Type 35B twin-seater roadster. The mechanic was essential, as he had to help the driver to operate the pumps

short-chassis racing cars being known as Brescias. Longer-chassis models were termed Brescias Modifiés. The 23 was the fastest light car available, and with a high axle ratio could manage 137km/h (85mph) at 3,800rpm. Four-wheel brakes were employed from 1925, and production of the Brescias ended in 1926.

The Bugatti company produced its first 8-cylinder car in 1922 as the Type 30, with the 2-litre (122cu in) single ohc which had 3 valves per cylinder mounted in the Type 23 chassis. There followed the immortal Type 35, which achieved practically all of its fame as a racing car. The Type 35A was the cheapest variant, having the Type 38 touring engine; the Type 35C was supercharged, and the 35T was the grand prix variant.

Bugatti also made the Type 43, the fastest production car of 1927. It had a 60 x 110mm (2.36 x 4.33in) straight-eight engine, which could manage a top speed of 177km/h (110mph). The Type 37 replaced the Brescia Modifié

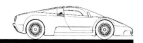

as a racing car but the Type 55 was an out and out sports car, having an engine which was virtually a supercharged twin-cam 2.3-litre (140cu in) with 16 valves. It is regarded by many as the finest of the Molsheim sports cars, although it did not appear until 1931. It preceded the last Bugatti sports car to be produced in any number, which was the Type 57. This appeared in 1934, powered by a 3.3-litre (201cu in) engine with two ohc producing 93kW (125bhp) and a top speed of 153km/h (95mph). The 57 chalked up Le Mans wins in 1937 and 1939, and did much to enhance the reputation of the company that was one of the most admired of the inter-war years.

Interwar America

In this country, so decidedly made for the motor car, production had soon outstripped that of all European countries combined. The automobile was embraced from the moment that factories in the east and the mid-west began turning out their runabouts,

cycle-cars, roadsters and many other innovative variants.

A vintage car is one constructed before the end of 1930, a date chosen specifically because of the trading depression that followed the stock market crash of 1929 in the USA, the shock waves of which vibrated around the world. The effect in America was to eliminate the small companies, undercapitalised companies or those which produced overpriced or inferior products. Those that were left to continue found the going far from easy. Manufacturers of luxury and sporting models were the first to suffer; mass producers struggled feverishly for sales by lowering prices, design departments concentrated on driver comforts and styling while striving to save on costs, and while some manufacturers contrived to build an honest automobile, others employed hideous gimmicks; the 1930s became an unloved decade.

Bugatti's beautiful 1934 Type 55 roadster

On the sports car scene, a number of embryonic companies had begun to create reputations but only one or two sports car manufacturers survived into the early 1930s. Production of the Stutz Bearcats and the Mercer Raceabouts ended in 1925, although the Stutz company did struggle into the next decade. The Paige Daytona had lasted for only a couple of years at the beginning of the 1920s, disappearing just before the Daniels Submarine Speedster, which ceased production in 1924. Thus there was little by way of a speedster available to the American public by 1925. There was the Jordan Playboy model, which was powered by a Continental straight-eight engine, and continued in production until 1929; there was also a Tomboy two-seater coupé, but Jordan was also history by 1931. The Kissel Motor Company, which had produced speedster models throughout the 1920s, also ceased production in 1931.

Stutz had stopped sponsored racing in 1928, although a privately-entered

17

four-seater tourer came second at Le Mans that year; it continued production of its Black Hawk speedster until 1932. A revived Bearcat had been introduced in 1931, with dohc and 4 valves per cylinder in a 5.2-litre (317cu in) engine which developed 116kW (156bhp). It had a wheelbase of 3.45m (11ft 2.5in) and a short-wheelbase version of 2.95m (9ft 8in), known as the Super Bearcat, was capable of 161km/h (100mph) in its drophead coupé version. Stutz halted production in 1933.

The two other American sports car manufacturers of the 1930s were part of the same combine, sharing both designers and engineers. One of these was Auburn, which reintroduced a speedster in 1932 which had a 6.8-litre (415cu in) Lycoming V12 and was available with a pointed boat-tail body. This was the only 12-cylinder car ever to be sold new in the USA for under $1,000. Production continued into 1934, and in the following year Auburn launched the extensive 851 range,

which included a new speedster with a top speed of 167km/h (104mph). This model went on to beat no fewer than 70 records at Bonneville, including 12 hours at over 161km/h (100mph), but with the end of 1936 also came the end of Auburn production.

The other partner in the combine with Auburn-Cord was Duesenberg, which produced little before 1936, when the partnership collapsed. Cord produced the striking Model 810 with wraparound grille and retracting headlights. It was powered by a V8 Lycoming engine of 4,729cc (289cu in) capacity, which drove the front wheels. Its top speed was 148km/h (92mph), although a supercharged option was available, which pushed the top speed to just over the 161km/h (100mph) mark.

The world slump had effectively annihilated the US sports car market and manufacturers, and Europe fared little better.

A 1933 Alfa Romeo 8C 2300 Spyder

Alfa leads the way

The most successful sports car manufacturer in Italy continued to be Alfa Romeo, which was the only one to produce really high-performance sports cars throughout the decade. In 1920 Alfa had produced the 20/30ES, with a 4,250cc (259cu in) engine that yielded 35.7kW (67bhp) at 2,600rpm. Its various body styles included a stripped two-seater, in one of which Enzo Ferrari came second in the 1922 Targa Florio. Alfa developed the RL range, which included the RLS and RLSS models, the latter being available from 1925 with a 61.8kW (83bhp) engine, which produced a top speed of about 137km/h (85mph).

The company also continued its success in the Targa Florio, with a first and second in 1923 and a second place in 1924 with the RL models, of which about 2,500 were produced between 1922 and 1927. Alfa also won the Mille Miglia in 1929, when the constructor also gained third place. This was the platform from which Alfa entered the

1930s. The company had produced the Tipo 6C and the Gran Sport by 1930, the latter winning the Mille Miglia again, the Coupe Boillot and a second place in the Targa Florio. Alfa's twin-cam 1,750cc (107cu in) continued in production until 1933, having been joined in 1931 by the 8C 2300, which was powered by a dohc straight-eight engine of 2,336cc (143cu in), which produced 97kW (130bhp) at 5,000rpm or 133kW (178bhp) in the racing versions. Maximum speeds of up to 177km/h (110mph) were claimed for various 8C versions, although the fastest, which competed in the Mille Miglia, was capable of 201km/h (125mph). The 6-cylinder dohc 2,309cc (141cu in) engined 6C 2300 arrived in 1934, and in 1935 evolved into the 2300B with all-round independent suspension. It was replaced by the 2500 in 1939. Perhaps the most exciting Alfa of the period was the 8C 2900, a very high-performance sports car which was derived from the grand prix Tipo B car. The 8C had a 2,905cc (177cu in) straight-eight dohc with twin turbo-chargers, producing an impressive 134kW (180bhp).

Alfa Romeo's roll of honour for the 1930s reads as follows:

Mille Miglia

1930	1st, Nuvolari; 2nd, Varzi; 3rd, Campari
1931	2nd, Campari
1932	1st, Borzacchini; 2nd, Trossi; 3rd, Scarfio
1933	1st, Nuvolari; 2nd, Castelbarco; 3rd, Taruffi
1934	1st, Varzi; 2nd, Nuvolari; 3rd, Chiron
1935	1st, Pintacuda; 2nd, Tadini; 3rd, Battaglia
1936	1st, Brivio; 2nd, Farina; 3rd, Pintacuda
1937	1st, Pintacuda; 2nd, Farina
1938	1st, Biondetti; 2nd, Pintacuda; 3rd, Dusio

Above: *lined up on Alfa's forecourt in Milan are the first three in the 1936 Mille Miglia*

Le Mans

1931	1st, Howe/Birkin
	Index, Howe/Birkin
1932	1st, Sommer/Chinetti; 2nd, Cortese/Guidotti
1933	1st, Nuvolari/Sommer; 2nd, Chinetti/Varent; 3rd, Lewis/Rose-Richards
	Index, Nuvolari/Sommer
1934	1st, Etancelin/Chinetti
1935	2nd, Stoffel/Helde

Targa Florio

1930	1st, Varzi
1931	1st, Nuvolari; 2nd, Borzacchini
1932	1st, Nuvolari; 2nd, Borzacchini
1933	1st, Brivio; 2nd, Balestrero; 3rd, Caracciola
1934	1st, Varzi; 2nd, Barbieri; 3rd, Magistri
1935	1st, Brivio; 2nd, Chiron

MILLE MIGLIA

Endurance road racing had come to prominence in the early years of the twentieth century, beginning with the prestigious city to city races within France. These were developed into cross-border races, but a series of spectacular crashes occurred in the 1903 Paris-Madríd race on the road to Bordeaux, which left both drivers and spectators crushed in a wreckage of tangled machinery. The resulting public outcry effectively banned long-distance inter-city races within Europe.

Even though events were switched from the open roads to circuits, so devastating was this disaster's effect upon motor racing that by the time of the French Grand Prix of 1926, only the pre-eminent Bugatti company responded to the sporting enthusiasts' demands to enter a works team, so low was the level of support for the sport among the manufacturers.

Nonetheless there was some impetus from a group of Milanese businessmen who had automobile interests, and were anxious to demonstrate the abilities and prowess of their products. Plans were formulated by the Brescia Automobile Club under the auspices of Count Mazotti, a team of journalists headed by Giovanni Canestrini, and the manufacturers, for a long-distance trial of Italian production cars. The intention was to publicise the Italian auto-mobiles' rugged reliability and speed.

A race was mooted initially to be run along the public roads from Brescia to Rome and back, but the authorities, mindful of the Paris-Madríd disaster, argued against it. They were overruled by Benito Mussolini, who was more interested in image, and brushed aside his officials' objections to sanction this 'thousand miles' race. The route and the regulations were soon devised, and the first Mille Miglia was run in 1927.

There was very little external com-petition in the early races, in fact on only three occasions did non-Italian cars prove to be the fastest. Mercedes-Benz won in 1931 and 1955, and in 1940 the title went to BMW. The Mercedes win of 1955 was the fastest-ever race, at an average speed of

Above: *Nuvolari is chaired aloft, following his 1930 victory in an Alfa Romeo 1750 Gran Sport*

Below: *Carlo Pintacuda stops to refuel during the 1935 race that he won with Della Stufa, in a Ferrari-modified Alfa Romeo P3 Type B*

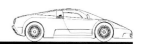

157.62km/h (97.96mph), the car being driven by Stirling Moss. The race was only ever won by one other non-Italian driver, Rudi Caracciola, the other Mercedes winner in 1931.

There were 78 starters for the first race, setting off at one-minute intervals from Brescia at dawn on the Saturday. They travelled down via Módena, Bologna, Firenze and Siena to Rome and back via Bologna and Verona, thus having to cross the Apennines twice during the day and night race. Many of the non-finishers had left the road rather than having come to a stop because of mechanical failures. Both for the first race and for the few that immediately followed, the control points were scenes of utter chaos especially at night time, exacerbated by the rain that famously dogged the event.

Above: *Giannino Marzotti in his Ferrari 195 Berlinetta Touring. This amateur in the double-breasted blue suit emerged triumphant and immaculate from the 1950 race. He* *was protected from the torrential rain by the car's closed body though when most of the other drivers crossed the finishing line they were soaked to the skin and covered in mud*

Below: *appalling weather also bedevilled the 1951 race, won by Gigi Villoresi and Piero Cassani in a 4-litre Ferrari Type 340 America*

The first race was won in an OM driven by Minoia and Moriando, at an average speed of 77km/h (47.9mph), but the event was dominated by Alfa Romeo for the first 12 years until 1938. This manufacturer attained 27 first-three placings out of the 36 available, including wins in all but the 1927 and 1931 events. The event was held only once between 1939 and 1946, on a closed circuit south of Brescia in 1940. In the 11 post-war races, Alfa Romeo took only a further four placings, while Ferrari dominated with 17.

The Alfa mastery had begun in 1928, with Campari and Ramponi driving a 1,500cc (91.5cu in) ohc. They also won in 1929, when there were 100 entrants, although horrific weather conditions forced them to change seven tyres. The race was won by Nuvolari at an average speed of 100km/h (62.41mph) in 1930, but the race in 1931 was one of the most outstanding. The lead changed hands several times, with Caracciola faster across the open plain but dropping to fourth place over the mountainous section, yet desperately holding on to win thanks only to the Mercedes' superior top speed.

Another of the great races was staged in 1934, during an absolute downpour,

through which Nuvolari duelled with Varzi in their Alfas, only to be surpassed by him just before the finish. Nuvolari, who had won the previous year, never succeeded again although he did achieve a second place once more, this time in a Cisitalia in 1947. He had led the race for about 1,528km (950 miles) through the traditional rainstorms, before seeing Biondetti pass in his Alfa.

Biondetti won again in 1948, but this time in a Ferrari, chased all the way by Fiat 1100s. He came back with another Ferrari in 1949 to complete a hat-trick, with Ferrari going on to take wins for the next four years.

Nuvolari died on 10 August 1953, and in his honour the 1954 race was diverted to Mantua. The effect of this was to make the Mille Miglia exactly the 1,609km (1,000 miles), for the first time. The field for that year totalled 374

Below: *this exceptional photo was taken by the journalist Louis Klemantaski in 1957, from the Ferrari 335 S driven by Peter Collins in the last Mille Miglia. The car ahead is the 315 S driven by Wolfgang von Trips, which finished second behind Piero Taruffi in another 315 S*

entrants, and the race was won by Antonio Ascari in a Lancia.

The race that stands as the epic Mille Miglia is that which ensued in 1955, when Stirling Moss demonstrated his considerable skill for ten hours at the wheel of a Mercedes 300SLR. He had been passed by Castellotti after he had spun off, but he pushed the Mercedes relentlessly until both the gearbox and the rear axle overheated. Between Parma and Piacenza his average speed topped 273km/h (170mph), while spotter planes struggled to keep up with him. He was pursued and harried all the way by Fangio. It was the race of his life; Moss was the first and only Englishman to win the race in the only non-Italian car to win in the post-war period, and at the fastest average speed for the race. Castellotti would win the race the following year.

The final Mille Miglia took place in 1957, largely because rising speeds and increased fatalities from accidents had led to increasing public demand for it to be discontinued, particularly after His Holiness the Pope spoke against it. This last race was won by Piero Taruffi, for the first time in 13 attempts. He led a Ferrari 1–2–3, just as Castellotti had done the previous year.

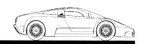

The Classic Age

Of course there were other Italian manufacturers, but their achievements pale into insignificance by comparison with those of Alfa. Lancia made a number of sports cars, including the Astura, which was introduced in 1931. This had a V8 2.6-litre (159cu in) engine of a narrow 19-degree angle, which could be cast as a monoblock. This developed 54kW (73bhp) at 4,000rpm, but was mutated into a 3-litre (183cu in) in 1933.

Fiat, a company not then regarded as a sports car producer, manufactured the Tipo 508S Balilla from 1933. This was an imitation of the Alfa Romeo 8C, and had a 995cc (61cu in) engine developing 27kW (36bhp).

Maserati was really a racing car producer, although the 8C-1100, 8C-1500 and 8C-2500 were available as sports models, all with straight-eight dohc engines.

Back in France, the dominating position of light sports car makers of the 1920s and the resultant wide choice had deteriorated, leaving a very thin selection for the enthusiast. Amilcar no longer made sports models

The Bugatti Type 57C coupé of 1937 was one of the great pre-war sports cars, and was capable of over 200km/h (124.3mph)

to any degree, and nor did its great rival of the 1920s, Salmson; the only French firm to make sports cars throughout the 1930s was Bugatti, which built on its successes of the previous decade.

There were the Type 40, 44 and 46 tourers in 1930, along with the Type 35 and 37 racing cars, and the Type 41 Royale. The limited-edition Type 46 was announced at the end of 1929; it was more of a luxury tourer than a sports car, but it had a 5,359cc (327cu in) straight-eight engine with a single ohc operating 3 valves per cylinder. The Type 46S was a supercharged model, with a top speed in excess of 145km/h (90mph). The Type 50 came out soon after the 46, and had an identical chassis and gearbox but, significantly for Bugatti, it had a 4,976cc (304cu in) engine inclined at 90 degrees, and operated by twin camshafts with 2 valves per cylinder. Both the Type 46 and the Type 50 were occasionally raced, but the most sporting Bugatti of

the decade was the Type 55, which replaced the Type 43 in 1932. It combined a twin-cam 2.3-litre (140cu in) engine, the same as that in the Type 51 race car, with the chassis of the Type 54. Its performance was an excellent 180km/h (112mph) top speed and it took 18 seconds to reach 0–129km/h (0–80mph). In the standard trim it was a two-seater roadster with sweeping wings and a rounded tail. It was to be the last of the sporting Bugattis, and production ceased in 1935. However in 1934, the company had launched the Type 57 tourer, with a dohc 3-litre (183cu in) engine, which developed 140bhp and had a maximum speed of 153km/h (95mph). The Type 57 was available in a variety of body styles, including a drophead coupé and two fixed-head coupés. The Type 57S was the sporting model, capable of 201km/h (125mph) and with a shorter chassis; when supercharged it was designated the 575SC. The Type 57 became the most raced Bugatti, winning at Le Mans in both 1937 and 1939.

Bugatti's rivals, Delahaye and Delage, had merged in the middle of the decade and produced a range of which the

largest was the 4.3-litre (262cu in), 8-cylinder D8/120. This new company scored some racing successes, including a win at Donington Park in the 1938 TT which was followed by a second place in the 1939 Le Mans.

Other cars of the era were the Talbot-Lago, and the Hotchkiss. The old Darracq company had disappeared, although some models continued to be marketed under that name in the UK. The company had been bought by Major Lago who introduced a new range of 6-cylinder ohv cars which in competition guise were known as the Lago Specials, and as such scored a 1–2–3 in the 1937 Sports Car Grand Prix at Montlhéry, followed by a victory in the 1937 TT Race.

The 3.5-litre (214cu in) Hotchkiss of 1933 was an extremely attractive model, and much cheaper than either the Darracq or the Delahaye, although it lacked nothing in performance. It was powered by a 6-cylinder 3,485cc (213cu in) ohv engine that developed 86kW (115bhp) to yield a maximum speed of 151km/h (94mph). This model was followed by a Super Sport in 1936, which had a shortened wheelbase and a power output tweaked to 93kW (125bhp). Hotchkiss was not a frequent visitor to the race track, concentrating more on rallies and winning the Monte Carlo in 1932, 1933, 1934 and 1939.

Meanwhile Germany had concentrated its efforts on the prestigious grands prix. State-aided Mercedes-Benz and Auto-Union racing teams absorbed the companies' resources, leaving little if anything for pure sports cars.

Mercedes had introduced super-charged engines at the 1922 Targa Florio, after which it developed a sports car with a limited production run. These examples were powered by 6-cylinder engines, and designed by Ferdinand Porsche; they led directly to the famous SS and SSK models. The Type K was launched in 1926, a fast tourer with a maximum speed of 161km/h (100mph). It was followed by the larger-engined Type S, which was not only a more refined and better-looking car, but had a top speed of 177km/h (110mph) which together with better handling and brakes took it on to score a 1–2–3 in the German Grand Prix of 1927,

followed by a 1–2 in 1928.

The Type SS appeared in 1928, with an engine now enlarged to 7 litres (427cu in). There were also the short-wheelbase version, the SSK, and the racing SSKL, which with a larger blower engine developed 224kW (300bhp). Success for the SS came in the form of a TT win in 1929, followed by victories in the Irish Grand Prix of 1930 and the German Grand Prix in 1931 for the SSK and in the same year in the Mille Miglia for the SSKL. Thus Mercedes-Benz entered the 1930s with a winning sporting line, and the SS models remained in production until 1933. The company produced a mixed bag of models with little direction or further success until the Type 500 K, which itself was replaced by the 540 K in 1936. Similar in appearance to the 500 K, the 540 K produced 134kW (180bhp), and had a top speed of 169km/h (105mph). Large and heavy, neither of these was designed for competition although both were beautiful machines which were usually offered in two-door body styles including a roadster, a coupé and a drophead coupé.

The Type 303 was offered with a 6-cylinder 1,173cc (71.5cu in) engine in 1933 by BMW, the engine size being increased to 1,490cc (90.9cu in) in the Type 315 of 1934. The two-seater sports model was designated Type 315/1 and was the forerunner of the famous Type 328, which had a top speed of about 161km/h (100mph) and achieved a second place on Index at the 1939 Le Mans. In 1940, after the Second World War had begun, it scored a first and third in the Mille Miglia.

In England, however, a wide range of sports cars continued to be offered into the 1930s, including a host of low-priced sports models which had been innovatively derived from the standard family saloons.

The MG Midget remained in production from 1928 to 1932, the year in which it scored an amazing 3–4–5–6–7 in its class at the Brooklands Double Twelve Hour Race. The formula for the Midget's astonishing success in both track and road racing was derived primarily from its engine. This was capable of cheap and extensive tuning,

and of sustaining high revs for long periods of time with reasonable reliability. It was allied to a hardiness produced by a combination of low weight, steering that was light and precise, and good tight springing.

Other British marques that were established during the 1920s and survived through the 1930s included Auto Carriers Ltd (AC), Alvis, Aston Martin, Austin, Frazer Nash, Lagonda and Riley.

AC experimented with a few engines after 1919, before choosing the 1.5-litre (91cu in) Anzani. This 6-cylinder sohc unit was enlarged to 1,991cc (121cu in), and then first appeared in 1922 in an AC chassis. Although these early two-seater ACs were raced, it was not until 1928 that the company offered its first sports model, the 16/66 Sports. The company produced several high-performance cars throughout the 1930s including the Ace, which first appeared in 1936. It continued developing its 6-cylinder block, which with 65 x 100mm (2.56 x3.9in) bore and stroke, and when fitted with a supercharger produced a top speed of 145km/h (90mph) in the 16/90 model.

Coventry-based Alvis produced the typical 1.5-litre (91cu in) British sports car of the period. Its 12/50, introduced in 1923, was completely on orthodox lines, using a pushrod 1,496cc (91cu in) engine.

At the end of the 1920s, Alvis changed its policy to concentrate on grands prix, which proved to be a short-lived flirtation and was soon reversed. The company then replaced the 12/50 and the 12/60 with a range of heavy small tourers, which grew both in size and in performance during the decade to the Second World War. The 1,496cc (91cu in) engine was retained for the smaller Firefly model, while the larger Firebird, introduced in 1935, had an 1,842cc (112cu in) engine. Even so, the car was too heavy to manage more than 116km (72mph).

Alvis used a 2,511cc (153cu in) engine in its Speed Twenty, which produced 65kW (87bhp) at 4,200rpm. It switched to independent leaf-spring suspension and introduced an all-synchromesh gearbox in mid-decade, together with another hike in capacity

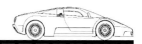

MERCEDES-BENZ 540 K

Country of origin: Germany
Date: 1936
Engine: inline 8-cylinder ohv, producing 85kW (115bhp) at 3,100rpm
Transmission: 4-speed manual
Wheels driven: rear
Capacity: 5,401cc (329.6cu in)
Bore & stroke: 88 x 111mm (3.46 x 4.37in)
Performance: maximum speed 168.3km/h (104.6mph); 0–96.5km/h (60mph) in 16.4 seconds
Dimensions: wheelbase 3.29m (10ft 9.5in); length 5.25m (17ft 2.5in); track 1.51m (4ft 11.5in) front, 1.5m (4ft 11in) rear
Steering: worm type
Kerb weight: 2,631kg (5,796lb)
Fuel: 120.6l (26.5gal/31.8US gal)
Suspension: independent coil springs and wishbones front; independent swing axles, double coil springs and lower-arm hydraulic dampers rear
Brakes: 4-wheel servo-assisted hydraulically-operated drums

Mercedes launched the 500 K in 1934, a luxury convertible widely regarded as the most beautiful Mercedes ever built. Two years later the company launched the 540 K; with its classical lines, it offered the ultimate in engineering perfection and comfort. It was acclaimed internationally as the supercharged sports car. The supercharged version produced 133kW (180bhp).

Although Daimler-Benz repeatedly attempted to woo a larger public with its small cars, the marque with the three-pointed star gained renown for its 6 and 8-cylinder models, both those with, and those without, supercharging. The supercharged era encompassed the legendary SS, SSK and SSKL, culminating in the 500 K and 540 K models, which have been some of the most exciting and coveted cars of all time.

Anyone who has seen the 540 K sports convertible, even only once, will know why the 1930s was one of the truly great eras in the history of the automobile. Today just five 500 Ks survive out of the 25 made.

Bottom: *a 1936 Mercedes-Benz 540 K (cabriolet) B; and below, a 540 SSK (sport special cabriolet), two-door coupé*

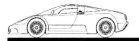

to 2,762cc (168cu in). The kerb weight was also increased so the two cancelled each other out, resulting in little if any increase to its performance which hovered at about 136km/h (85mph) top speed. The engine was increased again to 3,571cc (218cu in) in 1936, with the block being introduced into a Sport Twenty chassis to create the Sport Twenty-Five.

The first Aston Martin production cars had appeared in 1921, again with 1.5-litre (91.5cu in) sized engines. These were not particularly fast; they were expensive, but beautifully made and with excellent handling. Under the directorship of A.C. Bertelli, in 1927 the company produced another 1.5, which although produced in very small numbers remained in production until 1935 under such different model names as the International, Le Mans, Mark II and the Ulster. Some of these were raced, but with only modest success. The engine size was increased to 2 litres (122cu in) in 1936 with little effect on performance, but the marque has survived through to the present day and has provided us with much more in this post-war era.

Austin had built a team of 6-cylinder 9.7-litre (592cu in) grand prix cars as early as 1908, but it was not until 1924 that the company had produced its first real sports car. This was the Austin Seven sports , and was capable of a top speed of 84km/h (52mph). It remained in production for 12 years, and was available in various guises during that time including a supercharged 24.6kW (33bhp) incarnation. Although it was reasonably cheap, the Seven sports sold

only in small quantities whereas the 65 model, introduced in 1933 with a 17.1kW (23bhp) engine, was less expensive but sold considerably better. The latter was renamed the Nippy in 1935, which was the same year in which the 75, or Speedy, was first introduced. The Speedy remained in production for only a very short time, and the Nippy itself was discontinued in 1937.

Archie Frazer-Nash set up on his own in 1924, having split from the GN partnership he had formed with H.R. Godfrey. The new company produced its first car in 1925, using a 1.5-litre (91.5cu in) Anzani engine. The model remained in production right through to 1939, although a series of different power packs came into use. The Anzani was replaced by the ohv Meadows 4ED unit in 1929. An sohc 44.7kW (60bhp) Gough engine which Frazer Nash built itself was offered from 1934, along with a 6-cylinder dohc Blackburn engine which had one camshaft driven by chain and the other by helical gears from the first. All the engines employed were of 1.5 litres (91.5cu in), but the Blackburn was also offered in 1,657cc (101cu in) form. Although production was very small and always bespoke, the Frazer Nashes did race, though never as successfully as their rival British marques such as MG or Riley.

Having produced the elegant 113km/h (70mph) Redwing in 1919, Riley went on to produce the far better-known Nine in 1926. The power block at the heart of the Nine was an enterprising assembly with valve gear operated by short pushrods from two high cam-

shafts, the valves being set at 90 degrees in a hemispherical head.

The Nine model was developed into the Brooklands, an 1,100cc (67cu in) world-beater that not only won its class in the TT from 1928 to 1932 when it was held at Ards in Ireland, but also won the Irish Grand Prix outright in 1932. The car possessed outstanding acceleration and handling, but in 1934 it made way on the production line for the Imp, which was to prove an equally successful sports model. It was to be followed by two further successes, the 6-cylinder MPH and the 4-cylinder 1.5-litre (91.5cu in) Sprite.

Other sporting success came Riley's way with the Nine at Le Mans in 1935, when it won the 1.5-litre (91.5cu in) class and broke the 1,100cc (67cu in) class record by 14.5km/h (9mph). In 1935 and 1936, a Sprite powered by a 12/4 Model engine won the TT and when the French Grand Prix was run as a sports car race in 1936, Riley dominated the 1.5-litre (91.5cu in) class with 1–2–3–4 places.

The last season of Riley as an independent company was 1937/8, when the Sprite was the only sports model in production. After the Nuffield takeover in 1938, no more sports Rileys were made.

Another new sports car to emerge in the 1930s was the Morgan 4/4, the first four-wheeler from the company. It was a light sports car, powered by a 1,100cc (67cu in) Coventry-Climax engine. A drophead coupé version appeared in 1939 which was powered by a 1,267cc (77cu in) Standard Ten engine.

Wolseley produced the Hornet

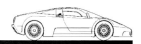

Above: *the SS Jaguar 100, with its windscreen folded down*

Below left: *a 1937 Riley Ulster Sprite*

Special at the beginning of the 1930s, and in 1935 followed it with the Hornet Special Fourteen. Neither car was truly reliable, exciting or even successful, although they were cheap. Unlike the SSI of 1931 designed by Swallow and built by Standard, the Hornet Special used a 2,054cc (125cu in) 6-cylinder Standard Sixteen engine, and was the forerunner of the 1936 four-door saloon SS Jaguars. These Jaguar saloons were followed by the two-seater SS Jaguar 100, which was low and wide with graceful flowing wings and a folding windscreen. It was a stunning model, though too underpowered for the enthusiast. It was given a 3.5-litre (213cu in) engine for 1938, which developed 93kW (125bhp) and pushed the top speed to above the all-important 161km/h (100mph) mark.

Singer had not produced sports cars during the 1920s, but developed one that was based on its successful Junior, launching the Nine in 1933. This

featured twin carburettors, a remote-control gearbox and hydraulic brakes, and was powered by a 972cc (59cu in) unit. After accidents in the 1935 TT, Singer withdrew from racing although the Nine remained in production until 1937.

Another model to feature an engine of less than a litre (61cu in) capacity was the Triumph Super Seven, which appeared in 1928 with a side-valve 832cc (51cu in) engine. The sports version followed in 1929, and despite being slightly heavier than the MG it was also slightly faster. When in racing trim it used a 747cc (46cu in) unit, but this had little success and was rapidly withdrawn. Triumph's only sporting model in 1931 was the Gnat, which was joined in 1933 by the Southern Cross; neither of which proved to be great racers, although they achieved some success in rallying.

Squire launched its first car in 1934. This also used the 1.5-litre (91.5cu in) Anzani engine, and although it had a beautiful two-seater body by Vanden Plas the price was prohibitive, and few were actually built.

Another model to use the 1.5-litre

(91.5cu in) 4-cylinder Meadows 4ED engine was that constructed by the HRG partnership, which was launched in 1935. It was a very light car, had a top speed of 133km/h (83mph) and was by no means unrealistically priced. The Meadows unit was replaced by a 1.5-litre (91.5cu in) ohc Singer in 1939. The company enjoyed some racing success, coming second in its class in both the 1937 and 1938 Le Mans races and winning the class in 1939.

The larger British cars came from Lagonda, Talbot and Bentley, with Lagonda producing its first sports car, the 2-litre (122cu in) Speed Model in 1928. This featured twin carburettors and had a maximum speed of 129km/h (80mph). This was followed by the 3-litre (183cu in), 6-cylinder model in 1929, which made way two years later for the 2-litre (122cu in) Continental. This in turn was followed by the 16/80 in 1932, which had a 6-cylinder Crossley engine. The 16/80 was withdrawn in 1934, after which Lagonda began to concentrate on bigger-engined cars, including both a 3.5-litre (213cu in) and a 4.5-litre (274cu in) model in that year. The latter, the M45, was powered

A 1932 MG Midget

by a 6-cylinder ohv Meadows engine and had the distinction of winning the 1935 Le Mans race at an average speed of 124km/h (77mph).

Lagonda launched the LG45 model in 1936, the design of which was overseen by William Owen Bentley who had joined the company in the previous year. The sporting version of the LG45 was the Rapide, which had a 112kW (150bhp) engine that produced a top speed of 174km/h (108mph). The LG6 appeared in 1938, and with V12 engines that yielded 164kW (220bhp) these cars managed very creditable third and fourth places in 1939 Le Mans.

The Talbot company had almost disappeared in the mid-1920s but launched its 90 model in 1930. This had a new 2,276cc (139cu in) 45kW (60bhp) engine, which was housed in the chassis of the previous year's Scout model. Two of these cars came second and third in that year's Le Mans, using engines already developed to 69kW (93bhp). They also won their class in the TT, and the Irish Grand Prix, in the same year. Talbots came third at Le Mans for the next two years, before going on to record many more racing successes. The same model names were retained through to 1935, when the

company collapsed and was bought by the Rootes Group; as the remaining parts were used, they were replaced by Humber equivalents and by 1939 they were no longer true Talbots.

This section concludes with a look at one of the great car makers of the period, Bentley. The reputation and image of the marque during the inter-war years is of a thunderous machine, bristling with muscle, tough and ruthless, being thrashed around the circuit at Brooklands.

The prototype 3-litre (183cu in) was laid down in 1919, and completed nine months later. After being exhibited at the Motor Show at London's Olympia, the car was immediately raced. Its first win was at Brooklands, and enabled Bentley to advertise the model for sale with a guaranteed 129km/h (80mph) and a five-year warranty. Deliveries began in 1921, and the following year Bentleys took second, fourth and fifth places in the TT, held for the last time on the Isle of Man. However, such success was tempered by the high price of the car, which deterred prospective buyers and pushed the company towards bankruptcy.

The creditors were kept at bay long enough for Bentley to offer the Six, in 1925. He announced the 4.5-litre (274cu in) two years later, and this was the model that won the Le Mans event in 1927. It also went on to win its class in the Six Hours Race at Brooklands in 1928 and the Brooklands 500 in 1929.

The Speed Six, however, remains the ultimate expression of Bentley's sports-car philosophy. The engine followed previous model style by being a fixed-head, long-stroke unit with an sohc running 8 bearings, driven by 3 coupling rods and operating 24 small-diameter valves through duralumin rockers to produce an output of 119kW (160bhp).

It was forced to retire after leading for nine hours when making its racing début at Brooklands in 1929, but this was to be a rare defeat. The Speed Six took Le Mans two years in succession, with a 1–2–3 in 1929 and a 1–2 in 1930 plus the Index in both years; the following year, Bentley had collapsed.

Under the ownership of Rolls-Royce, new Bentleys appeared in 1933. A sports tourer was one of the body styles available, but it was never intended for racing although some examples were privately entered.

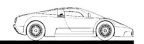

CHRONOLOGY 1898–1939

1898 A world speed record of 63.14km/h (39.24mph) is set by Comte Gaston de Chasseloup-Laubat.
The first races are held in Germany and Belgium, and the first city-to-city race is held, from Paris to Amsterdam and back.

1899 E.R. Sewell, a Daimler test driver, becomes the first British driver to be killed.
Paris is firmly established as the centre of the automobile world, with the Paris motor show, the Paris to Ostend race and the Tour de France, which was won this year by Panhard at an average speed of 48.6km/h (30.3mph) for the 2,172km (1,350 miles).
Camille Jenatzy sets a new speed record of 105.9km/h (65.79mph).

1900 The first fine for drunken driving is imposed by the Dublin Police Court, on Mr Kelly for £1.00.
The first circuit race, the Cours du Catalogue, is held at Mélun.
New cars are launched by Napier, Lancaster, De Dion, Wolseley, Panhard and Peugeot.
Gottlieb Daimler dies.

1901 The discovery of Tarmacadam, which transforms the world's roads.
French car production is booming, with 1,500 cars and voiturettes being produced and Darracq claiming sales of 1,000 for its Voiturettes, two-thirds of the market.
The American Locomobile light steam car is proving popular.

1902 Vauxhall and Singer announce their first cars.
L. Serpollet, a Frenchman, sets a new speed record of 120.7km/h (75mph).
Cadillac builds its first car, having formed the company a year earlier.

1903 The first British Motor Show, held by the Society of Motor Manufacturers and Traders.
Flourishing marques now include Darracq and Panhard in France, Mercedes and Opel in Germany, Oldsmobile in America and Wolseley and Napier in Britain.

1904 The UK speed limit is raised to 32km/h (20mph).
Rolls and Royce join forces. Armstrong Whitworth and Rover also enter the fray.
Henry Ford races to a new land speed record of 147km/h (91.37mph) in his 999 car at Lake St Clair.

1905 The Automobile Association holds its first meeting.
Herbert Austin sets up his factory in Longbridge.

1906 The first French Grand Prix is staged at the Circuit de la Sarthe at Le Mans. It is won by a Renault.
The USA becomes the largest car maker; previously it had been France.
The Targa Florio is first run in Sicily over three laps of the 148.82km (92.48-mile) circuit.

1907 The world's first purpose-built race circuit opens at Brooklands. A Napier wins the inaugural race in front of about 13,500 spectators.
Isotta Fraschini and Itala both launch new high-performance sports cars.

1908 The Ford Model T goes on sale, priced at $900.00.
General Motors is formed by the merger of Buick with Oldsmobile.
The first Lancias of four and six cylinders are revealed.

1909 Daimler and Lancaster merge.
Austin and Swift announce a joint-production 5.2kW (7hp) engine.
Lacoste and Battmann design the Simplicia frameless car.
British motor vehicle registration reaches 100,000.

1910 The Scottish-built Argyll is the first car with 4-wheel brakes.
Charles Rolls, co-founder of Rolls-Royce, is killed in an air crash.

1911 Cadillac introduces electric lights and starters.
The first running of the 500-mile Sweepstakes at Indianapolis.
The first Monte Carlo rally is held.
Lagonda launches its 14.9 and 22.4kW (20 and 30hp) cars of four and six cylinders respectively, just two of 70 models now on offer in the UK.

1912 Triplex safety glass is established in Britain, although it was a French invention, patented in 1910.
WRM Motors of Cowley, Oxford, is registered with its first managing director being William Morris.

1913 William Morris builds his first car, the 'bullnose'.
Bugatti designs the Peugeot 'bébé', without a gearbox.
A Peugeot wins the Indianapolis 500.
Speed merchant Camille Jenatzy dies.
Percy Lambert drives his 18.6kW (25hp) Talbot 166.78km (103 miles 1,470 yards) in one hour.

1914 Cadillac introduces the world's first water-cooled V8.
The Motor Show at London's Olympia is suspended as war looms.
The Swift light car and the 11.2kW (15hp) Singer make their débuts.
Mercedes wins the French Grand Prix.

1915 The Stutz Bearcat is launched.
Britain applies a 33.3 per cent import duty on cars and parts, and doubles petrol duty.

1916 The first 12-cylinder engine is made by Packard, and mechanical windscreen wipers by Willys-Knight.

1917 Rootes Ltd is registered and becomes the biggest UK car distributor by 1925.

1918 The First World War ends.
Chevrolet joins General Motors.

1919 The UK Ministry of Transport is established.
André Boillot wins the Targa Florio.
Armstrong, Whitworth, Siddeley and Deasy merge.
Bentley Motors is registered.

1920 Ferodo component makers is established.
Bugatti wins its first race, the International
Voiturette Race at Le Mans, with a Type 13.
Sunbeam, Talbot and Darracq merge to form STD
Motors.

1921 Tax discs are introduced in the UK, where the buyer
now has a choice of 192 models available.
Hydraulic brakes are first used on a grand prix car,
a Duesenberg, which won the French race.

1922 The first mechanical headlight-dipping system is
devised.
Mercedes introduces the supercharger to European
racing in the Targa Florio.
The Austin Seven is launched.

1923 There are now one million registered vehicles on
UK roads.
The first Le Mans 24-Hour race is held.
The Lancia Lambda is launched, pioneering unitary
construction.

1924 Bentley wins its first Le Mans.
The first 24-hour Spa Race for touring cars is held.
Triumph pioneers 4-wheel Lockheed hydraulic
brakes in Britain.

1925 Ford notches up its quarter-millionth British-built
car.
Racing driver Antonio Ascari dies in a crash at the
French Grand Prix.

Germany shows the first car phone.
'Old Number One' is registered and thus the MG
sports car is born.
General Motors acquires a controlling interest in
Vauxhall and Opel.

1926 Britain has traffic lights for the first time.
Brooklands hosts the first British Grand Prix.
Mercedes and Benz merge to form Daimler-Benz.
The 'car for kings', the Bugatti Type 41 Royale, is
launched.

1927 A world land speed record of 327.98km/h
(203.841mph) is set by Henry Segrave, in a
Sunbeam.
The first running of the Mille Miglia.

1928 The Duesenberg Model J makes an impressive
début at the New York Salon on 1 December, one
day before the Ford Model A is unveiled.

1929 The last car to have solid tyres is produced.
Henry Segrave in his *Golden Arrow* takes the world
land speed record to 371.68km/h (231mph).
Bentleys score 1–2–3–4 at Le Mans.

**Below: *MG's Old Number One, which is now on
exhibition at the British Heritage Motor Centre,
Gaydon***

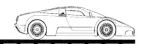

1930 In a race from Calais to the Riviera, a Rover Light
Six beats the Blue Train.
Third-party insurance is ushered into the UK by the
Road Traffic Act.
US car production reaches five and a half million.
1931 The UK Highway Code is introduced.
Donald Healey wins the Alpine Cup, in addition to
the Monte Carlo rally.
Ford opens its Dagenham factory.
1932 Sir Arthur Sutherland buys Aston Martin.
1933 The first all-synchromesh gearbox to be fitted as
standard is included on the Alvis Speed Twenty.
Sir Henry Royce dies.
Sir Malcolm Campbell sets a new land speed record
of 438.1km/h (272.26mph), in *Bluebird*.
1934 Deliveries begin of the Bugatti Type 57.
Citroën launches the front-wheel driven Traction
Avant, and Mercedes the 500 K.
Alfa wins at Le Mans for the fourth year running,
while Hotchkiss wins the Monte Carlo rally for the
third time running.
1935 The Ford Model Y is launched, priced at £100.
Percy Shaw invents reflective road studs (cat's eyes).
Britain acquires the display L-plate, a 48km/h
(30mph) speed limit, broken white lines along the
centre of the highway and pedestrian crossings
guarded by Belisha beacons.

The MG SA is launched.
Tazio Nuvolari wins the German Grand Prix in an
Alfa.
Sir Malcolm Campbell pushes his land speed record
to 484km/h (301mph).
1936 Mercedes produces its first diesel car, the 250D,
and Jaguar the SS100.
Jensen unveils its first car.
1937 Speedometers become compulsory on all British cars.
Bernd Rosemeyer takes the British Grand Prix in his
works Auto Union.
1938 John Cobb breaks the world land speed record at
563.5km/h (350.2mph) but George Eyston betters
that with his *Thunderbolt* at a speed of 575.2km/h
(357.5mph). German Bernd Rosemeyer loses his life
while attempting to break this record on an
Autobahn.
1939 Brooklands holds its last race on 9 August.
Triumph is rescued from receivership.
The Citroën Six and Singer Roadster appear.
Petrol rationing is introduced in Britain. There are a
record three million-plus vehicles on Britain's roads,
of which two million are cars.
Germany cuts the numbers of models available
from 55 to 23.

Below: *a 1936 Mercedes-Benz Type 500 K roadster*

ALFA ROMEO 6C 2500 SS

Country of origin: Italy
Date: 1939–51
Engine: dohc inline 6-cylinder with 2 valves per cylinder, producing 82kW (110bhp) at 4,800rpm
Transmission: 4-speed manual
Wheels driven: rear
Capacity: 2,443cc (149cu in)
Bore & stroke: 72 x 100mm (2.8 x 3.9in)
Performance: maximum speed 165km/h (102.5mph)
Dimensions: wheelbase 2.7m (8ft 10in); length not known; width not known; height not known; track 1.45m (4ft 9.1in) front, 1.47m (4ft 9.8in) rear
Steering: not known
Kerb weight: 1,400kg (3,087lb)
Fuel: 80l (17.6gal/21.1US gal)
Suspension: coil springs and trailing arms front; independent swing axles and longitudinal torsion bars rear
Brakes: drums front and rear
Compression ratio: 8 : 1

Anonima Lombardo Fabbrica Automobili (Alfa) built its first car in 1910, with the industrialist Nicola Romeo taking over the company in 1915. However, cars formed only a small part of its output, which was concentrated on aero engines.

During the inter-war years Alfa Romeo was the dominant racing marque, winning ten of the twelve pre-war Mille Miglia races, the Le Mans endurance race for four years in a row, and dozens of grands prix.

Alfa's 1938 racers continued succeeding on the racetrack after the Second World War,

although by then the company had decided to become a volume manufacturer. Its heavily-bombed factory began a stop-gap production in 1947 of the 6C. This had originally been designed in 1939, and now was offered in several body styles, most of which were executed by Touring.

Production of the model lasted until 1952, and Alfa managed to produce almost 1,500 units. It was the last of the true bespoke Alfas; its place in the production line was taken by the 1900. This was Alfa's first post-war design, of which Sprint and Super Sprint sports versions were to be produced between 1954 and 1958.

Below: *an authentic Touring-bodied Tipo 6C 2500 SS and*, above, *with 1940s coachwork by Carrosserie de Mola, Belgium*

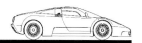

MODERN SPORTS CARS

This chapter concerns the very different world environment that prevailed after the conclusion of the Second World War, and through 100 models traces the development of the industry, from a desperate lack of resources to the ultimate supercars.

Neither the time, the raw materials nor the investment finance were available to develop new models after the Second World War, so slightly modified versions of pre-war models were pushed back into production. Not surprisingly, these were frequently and accurately criticised for their obsolete design as well as poor-quality finish and unreliability. There was a mixture of dull-looking body shapes in drab colours, and chassis that were to linger on well into the 1950s.

However, Jaguar was one of the first manufacturers to show some initiative and innovation, launching the XK120 in 1948. A combination of outstanding looks and a superb 3.4-litre (207cu in) engine made this two-seater with the aluminium roadster body an instant hit at the Earl's Court Motor Show. Its elegant lines are said to have been inspired by the pre-war Bugatti chassis, and on entering production it became the fastest production model available. After the first batch had been delivered, Jaguar had problems in keeping abreast of demand. A fixed-head coupé version was unveiled in 1951, and a drop-head version in 1953.

Also during the early 1950s, Donald Healey obtained a number of Austin components from which he built a two-seater sports car. He carried out the early trials in Belgium, and was so

This 1952 Jaguar XK120 coupé covered a distance of 27,112km (16,851 miles) in 168 hours of continuous driving, at an average speed of 177.49km/h (110.31 mph)

encouraged by the results that when he returned to London he exhibited the car at the Earl's Court Motor Show. There it met with immediate stardom; so impressed was Leonard Lord, then managing director of the British Motor Corporation (BMC), that he concluded a deal with Healey on the spot. The Austin-Healey 100 was born, and on entering production in 1953 became an instant success as the public snapped up over 10,000 units. Production was switched from West Bromwich to Abingdon in 1957, and there the much-loved and well-named Frogeye made its début the following year. This sold almost 50,000 units, before the Sprite II arrived in 1961.

Healey's real masterpiece, however, was the 3000; launched in 1959 with a 92kW (124bhp) 3-litre (183cu in) engine, it went through three versions, selling 40,000 units. It was then axed in its heyday, discarded when the design needed only tweaking to meet increased safety standards.

The fledgling French car industry,

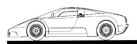

which had been a world leader at the beginning of the century, had lost many of its renowned marques. They had been killed off by 1954, through a combination of fiscal measures and old-fashioned design. The one model that bucked the trend was the 4.5-litre (274cu in) De Soto V8-engined Vega, produced by Forges et Ateliers de Construction d'Eure et de Loire SA (Facel). The engine fed its 134kW (180bhp) through a two-speed automatic transmission. The model was developed and improved, emerging as the HK500 in 1959 with a beautifully-tuned 268kW (360bhp) 6.3-litre (384cu in) engine. Sadly, Facel went the way of many of its compatriot companies, being declared bankrupt in 1962.

American muscle

At the same time, across the Atlantic Detroit was stirring. Having attracted its clientèle by the wild overstatement of its packaging, its attention was now diverted to what was under the hood. Out went those famous fins, to be replaced by a more solid sculptural styling. In went the big block; five litres soon gave way to six, six to seven and the American V8s of the 1960s flaunted that essential swagger to grab the world's interest and imagination.

Chevrolet had introduced its small-block V8, with 4,343cc (256cu in) capacity, in the mid-1950s but by the early 1960s the horsepower race was really dominant, boosted by cheap fuel and straight roads. Chrysler offered 6,558cc (400cu in), Chevrolet 6,706cc (409cu in), Dodge and Plymouth 6,771cc (413cu in); by 1963, all the big manufacturers were offering 6,982 or 7,000cc (426 or 427cu in) top options, with the ultimate muscle car having a 6,982cc (426cu in) 426 Hemi (hemispherical-head engine).

The Chevrolet Corvette, which had

The Ford Thunderbird was launched in 1955, powered originally by a V8 that was to increase in size and power as the US mid-fifties horsepower race went full bore

been launched in 1953, by 1958 had also evolved into a 5.7-litre (348cu in) monster with an 8-cylinder engine. It was transmuted into the Sting Ray in 1963. Essentially it was really a different car, with epoch-making features such as a fibreglass body with retractable headlights and a highly-developed fuel-injected 5,359cc (327cu in) V8 engine that produced 268kW (360bhp). It was built for speed, and also delivered reliability.

With the imported Volkswagen 'Beetle' eating into Detroit's profits, Ford took a gamble and transformed the lowly Falcon into a sporty Mustang in 1964 thereby creating overnight a new market for Barracudas, Camaros, Cougars, Challengers, Firebirds and Javelins to come.

America produced still more thanks to Carroll Shelby, the flamboyant Texan who had shoehorned a Ford V8 into a British AC roadster to create the legendary racing Ford AC Cobras. Unimpressed by the performance of the showroom Mustang, he then set about

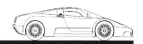

changing just about everything on it that could be unbolted. He transformed a blancmange into a state of the art street racer powered by a raucous 4,727cc (289cu in) V8 Windsor engine.

Chevrolet unveiled the Camaro in September, 1966. It was of pony car proportions, with a 2.74m (9ft) wheelbase, and was available as either a coupé or a convertible. It offered a wide range of power units and an extensive list of options, was curvier and had cleaner styling than the Ford Mustang. Originally Chevrolet offered a sport edition, but within months made eyes pop by launching a big-block 6,490cc (396cu in) V8, tuned to either 242 or 279kW (325 or 375bhp).

Camaro production ended in 1970, the same year in which Plymouth first offered the Road Runner Superbird. This was conceived by the company as a limited-edition model for homologation by the National Association for Stock Car Racing (NASCAR). It was produced only for that year, and all race versions were powered by Hemi engines.

Europe's power race

In mainland Europe, Lamborghini was about to launch its Miura at the 1966 Geneva Motor Show. This was a compromise between a street car and an all-out racer, following the tradition of being mid-engined. This had been a feature of all of the fastest sports-racing cars since 1959, when John Cooper had introduced the open-cockpit Monaco, and a design practice of Ferrari seen in its 246 SP and 250P cars of 1961 and 1963. Together with the 250LM coupé, these had taken the honours at Le Mans in 1963, 1964 and 1965.

The Miura also had the Lamborghini trademark of a short wheelbase, and a Bertone body design. It was a truly innovative masterpiece, the first real exotic and indeed a supercar. Ferrari's answer was its own mid-engined, roadgoing supercar, the 512 Berlinetta Boxer.

Maserati joined the fray with the Ghibli in 1966, focussing on road cars rather than competition cars after entering into a deal with Citroën in January of 1968. The Ghibli was beautifully styled by Giorgio Giugiaro, and remains perhaps the most stunning of all of the Maserati road cars.

Road and Track magazine tested the Ferrari 365 GTB/4 in 1970. This had been dubbed the Daytona by the world's press, who declared it to be 'an elegant machine that is unsurpassed in modern GT cars'. Ferrari's fabulous front-engined Berlinetta concept had evolved during 1967, when the 3.3-litre (201cu in) quad-cam 275 GTB/4 model was just being introduced into the high-performance car market. The car that was to be the 365 GTB/4 Daytona was developed by Maranello with its typical rapidity, and subsequently launched at Paris in 1968.

Aston Martin had offered its DB6 at the London Motor Show in 1965, a recognisable offspring of the DB4 and DB5 models but with a different upswept tail which gave a spoiler effect.

A 1968 4.7-litre (287cu in) Maserati Ghibli Berlinetta

Its other identifying features were the rounded rear window and a split bumper. However, the DB6 retained the 4-litre (244cu in) DB5 engine, which enabled it to reach 0–96.5km/h (60mph) in just six seconds, with a top speed of 241.4km/h (150mph).

Following the trend to more litres and more cylinders, in 1969 Aston Martin offered the DBS with a 5.3-litre (213 cu in) V8 engine producing 268kW (360bhp). The Vantage model (a designation used for many years by this manufacturer to signify a tuned version of a standard engine) produced kW326 (438bhp) and was capable of 273km/h (170mph).

The company was sold by David Brown in 1972, after which the DB designation was dropped, and the cars became known as the V8 Vantage, Volante, and Vantage Volante until the launch of the stunning new DB7 at the 1996 Geneva Motor Show.

Also in the UK, but on a completely different scale, is the Morgan car company. It was founded in 1910 and introduced the 4/4 in 1936; this was a model that to all intents and purposes is still being produced today. The Plus

Eight was introduced in 1968, powered by a Rover 3.5-litre (213cu in) V8. Since then, the company has gradually refined both power and performance by way of fuel injection, a 5-speed gearbox and rack and pinion steering. Like the other long-lived Morgans, the Plus Eight remains a modern car in vintage clothing; truly a car in a class of its own, and in the spirit of open-top motoring.

A spectacular array of cars was provided for us in the 1970s, with the Countach from Lamborghini, the Berlinetta Boxer from Ferrari, the rallying Stratos from Lancia, and a pair of classic Porsches that arrived mid-decade, the 911 Turbo and the 928.

Ferrari launched the Pininfarina-styled 365 GT4BB (Berlinetta Boxer) in 1973. It was followed by the 512 BB, which sparked off a supercar race for production with Lamborghini which had drawn first blood by launching the Countach in 1971. The 512 BB was the first Ferrari not to have a Vee engine, having instead a flat-12 derived from the company's Formula One boxer engine. Both rivals claimed 283kW (380bhp), but the Countach was

quicker away from the lights. Ferrari increased the BB's engine capacity to 4,942cc (301cu in) in 1976, and then introduced the BBi variant with Bosch Jetronic fuel injection. Lamborghini countered by increasing its car's capacity to 4,754cc (290cu in) and it was still quicker, reaching 0–96.5km/h (60mph) in a decreased time of 4.8 seconds. Ferrari responded with the Testarossa, but even by 1985 the Countach was still the fastest car to have been road-tested by the specialist British autocar press, having a top speed of 286km/h (178mph). The issue was not speed alone; what Pininfarina did for Ferrari, the Bertone studios did for Lamborghini, and the Countach was arguably their best.

The Lancia Stratos was another Bertone confection, a mid-engined styling exercise with a two-seater coupé being created around a simple steel monocoque and a fibreglass body. It was first exhibited in 1970 but not put into production until 1972, and then with a 2,418cc (147cu in) Ferrari Dino V6 engine. Just 500 were built, but these cars' reputation is second to none.

Porsche introduced the formidable 911 Turbo, one of the very first of the European turbocharged cars, in the mid-1970s. It was originally designated the Carrera 3.0, with power supplied by a 3-litre (183cu in) engine that produced a top speed of 260km/h (162mph). Years later, a modified Porsche 911 Turbo was clocked at 347.5km/h (216mph) on a German Autobahn. Apart from the French Alpine, the 1964-born 911 was the only high-performance car of the era to keep its power in its tail.

At the same time as increasing the engine capacity of the 911 Turbo, Porsche also launched the 928, another long-lived model but this time front-engined. It had a superb 4.5-litre (274cu in) fuel-injected sohc V8, with one camshaft per bank of cylinders. It was a Stuttgart masterpiece, with a

Left: *Lancia's Stratos goes rallying*

Below: *the Jaguar XJ220 introduced a new breed of supercars*

build quality, practicality and reliability that none of its rivals could match.

The remarkable Audi Quattro arrived with the 1980s, and was to bow out just as the first of a new breed of supercars appeared to crown this final decade in the century of sports cars.

In the middle of the decade was the rebirth of the Marcos, a marque founded in 1959 which disappeared in 1971 only to rise again ten years later. Initially offering only kits, the company launched the Mantula in 1984. It was a stylish two-seater race-bred model, reminiscent of the 1960s.

The French MVS company also came and went and returned again in the 1980s, with its tempting Venturi two-seater coupé. This eventually evolved, in 1989, into the Venturi 280 turbo-charged cabriolet with a unique Transcoupé two-piece roof.

The same decade also saw the Porsche 959, bristling with technology, become the world's fastest production car although it lost the company money. Ferrari marked its fortieth

anniversary with the dramatic-looking F40, with its large integral rear spoiler and a short-stroke variation of the 3-litre (183cu in) quattrovalvole V8 with twin IHI turbochargers. Perhaps it never really fulfilled Ferrari's dreams, but all of the planned production run of 450 were sold prior to the start of manufacture. This car also stirred up the world market for supercars with this sales success, and laid down the criteria for the other manufacturers to match which is what the 1990s have been all about.

Dodge, Jaguar, Bugatti, McLaren and Ferrari again all launched breathtaking supercars, while in their wake came a new clutch of true sports cars that deliver all they promise. While we recognise this second golden age of the sports car, we must also consider the genre's whole history, which is one of invention, innovation, dreams and disasters. The single greatest challenge for a new millenium is to extend the technology, conserve our environment, and still have fun.

MG TC

Country of origin: UK
Date: 1945
Engine: 4-cylinder with pushrod-operated overhead valves and twin SU carburettors, producing 40.6kW (54.4bhp) at 5,200rpm
Transmission: 4-speed manual
Wheels driven: rear
Capacity: 1,250cc (76.3cu in)
Bore & stroke: 66.5 x 90mm (2.6 x 3.5in)
Performance: maximum speed 125.5km/h (78mph); 0–96.5km/h (60mph) in 22.7 seconds
Dimensions: wheelbase 2.388m (7ft 10in); length 3.543m (11ft 7in); width 1.422m (4ft 8in); height 1.346m (4ft 5in); track 1.143m (3ft 9in) front and rear
Kerb weight: 822.2kg (1,811lb)
Fuel: 61.4l (13.5gal/16.5US gal)
Suspension: semi-elliptic springs front and rear; beam axle front, live rear axle
Brakes: 228mm (9in) drums front and rear
Compression ratio: 7.5 : 1

The firm started as Morris Garages, run by Cecil Kimber, and in 1928 it produced the trendsetting M-type Midget sports car before going on to produce a whole range of sports and sports-racing cars during the 1930s.

Immediately after the Second World War, sports cars followed the trend set by manufacturers of saloons, that is, they were pre-war designs tweaked to compensate for a shortage of materials. Thus the TC was no more than a 1930s TB, albeit 101mm (4in) wider, retaining its double-hump cowl, cutaway doors, slab-mounted

fuel tank, rear-mounted spare tyre, fold-flat screen, 482mm (19in) wire wheels and swept clamshell bumpers. Fewer than 400 TBs had been built before the War shut down production at the Abingdon plant.

Production of the TC lasted from 1945 to 1949, during which time just over 10,000 units were produced. It was the beautifully-balanced TC that, together with the Jaguar XK120, started the sports car boom in North America after the War. Initially introduced by returning GIs, and then officially by Motor Sport Inc of New York City, the MG TC had an influence on Americans far out of proportion to its production.

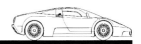

CISITALIA 202 GRAN SPORT

Country of origin: Italy
Date: 1947
Engine: inline 4-cylinder with 8 overhead valves and a single carburettor producing 55.9kW (75bhp) at 5,500rpm
Transmission: 4-speed manual
Wheels driven: rear
Capacity: 1,089cc (66.4cu in)
Bore & stroke: 68 x 75mm (2.7 x 2.9in)
Performance: maximum speed 201.1km/h (125mph)
Dimensions: wheelbase 2.398m (7ft 10.4in); length 4.153m (13ft 7.5in); width 1.45m (4ft 9.1in); height 1.359m (4ft 5.5in); track 1.257m (4ft 1.5in) front, 1.247m (4ft 1.1in) rear
Steering: worm and sector
Kerb weight: 662.8kg (1,460lb)
Fuel: 90.8l (20gal/24US gal)
Suspension: leaf springs front and rear
Brakes: drums front and rear
Compression ratio: 7.5 : 1

Piero Dusio founded Consorzio Industriale Sportivo Italia (Cisitalia) to produce a variety of goods. After the Second World War, the company entered the automobile market when he hired the Fiat engineer Dante Giacosa to design a monoposto racing car. Dusio dreamed of creating the very first one-design racing class, with Tazio Nuvolari as his driver.

In 1947 Dusio's race chief, Piero Taruffi, won the Italian championship in a Cisitalia roadster. In that ground-breaking year, Dusio also sent a chassis to the small 'Pinin' Farina firm.

That 1947 chassis became the 202, was awarded the grand prize at the Coppa d'Oro show at Lake Como,

and went on to be the star of the show at the Paris motor show. Today the Cisitalia 202 is on exhibition at the New York Museum of Modern Art, where it has been since its selection by Arthur Drexler in 1951, representing design excellence.

Dusio had a full order book in 1947, and he decided also to embark on a world-conquering grand prix car. He ransomed Ferdinand Porsche for the purpose from the French Government, which had been holding him on Nazi war crime charges.

Porsche overspent disastrously to produce only one, uncompetitive, model and the venture failed. Dusio mortgaged his business to support the project, but by 1949 Cisitalia was bankrupt and Dusio accompanied the remnants of the firm to Argentina.

Below: *the Cisitalia 202 Gran Sport* and left, *Dusio's 1947/49 12-cylinder supercharged monoposto racer that never raced is unveiled at the Turin motor show*

JAGUAR XK120

Country of origin: UK
Date: 1948
Engine: dohc inline 6-cylinder with 12 overhead valves and twin SU carburettors, producing 119.3kW (160bhp) at 5,100 rpm
Transmission: 4-speed manual
Wheels driven: rear
Capacity: 3,442cc (210cu in)
Bore & stroke: 83 x 106mm (3.3 x 4.2in)
Performance: maximum speed 202.7km/h (126mph); 0–96.5km/h (60mph) in 12 seconds
Dimensions: wheelbase 2.591m (8ft 8in); length 4.394m (14ft 5in); width 1.562m (5ft 1.5in); height 1.334m (4ft 4.5in); track 1.295m (4ft 3in) front, 1.27m (4ft 2in) rear
Steering: recirculating ball
Kerb weight: 1,325kg (2,919lb)
Fuel: 68.2l (15gal/18US gal)
Suspension: independent torsion bars front; semi-elliptic springs rear
Brakes: drums front and rear
Compression ratio: 8 : 1

This first post-war classic was produced from 1948–54.It was a two-seater roadster, and proved successful as the result of Jaguar getting both the style and the price right. Bill Lyons had founded the company in 1922, built custom bodies from 1927, and introduced the first Standard-based SSI in 1931. After the War, the company was renamed Jaguar Cars Ltd, and resumed with the production of the 1930s 1°, 2° and 3°-litre saloon models, before launching the Mark V and the XK120 Roadster in 1948. The XK120 fixed-head coupé was introduced in 1951, and the drop-head coupé in 1953.

The XK120 made its début at the Earls Court show in October,

1948. It was staggeringly beautiful, and powered by a new 3.4-litre engine that produced 119.3kW (160bhp) and a guaranteed 194km/h (120mph) straight out of the show-room. Honours and titles soon came its way, with Stirling Moss winning the 1950 Tourist Trophy. In 1953 at Jabbeke, Belgium, a modified XK120 attained a top speed of 277.58km/h (172.412mph).

Production of all models topped 12,000 and by the time the company moved to its new (and still current) headquarters in 1950 at Browns Lane, Allesley, Coventry, nearly 90 per cent of its output was being exported.

Bottom: Ian Appleyard's winning XK120 in the International Alpine Rally

PORSCHE 356

Country of origin: Austria
Date: 1948
Engine: air-cooled ohv mid-mounted flat 4-cylinder with twin carburettors, producing 29.8kW (40bhp) at 4,000rpm
Transmission: 4-speed manual
Wheels driven: rear
Capacity: 1,131cc (69cu in)
Bore & stroke: 73.5 x 64mm (2.89 x 2.5in)
Performance: maximum speed 135km/h (84mph)
Dimensions: wheelbase 2.108m (6ft 11in); length 3.874m (12ft 8.5in); width 1.66m (5ft 5in); height 1.295m (4ft 3in); track 1.29m (4ft 2.8in) front, 1.252m (4ft 1.3in) rear
Steering: worm and peg
Kerb weight: 839kg (1,850lb)
Fuel: 54.1l (11.9gal/14.3US gal)
Suspension: upper and lower trailing arms (anti-roll bar from 1954) front, swing axles with trailing arms at rear
Brakes: hydraulic on all four wheels
Compression ratio: 7 : 1

Although the Ferdinand Porsche engineering consultancy had been set up in 1931, the first car to bear its founder's name was the Porsche 356. It was created by his son, Ferry, in collaboration with Karl Rabe.

The 356 was a Volkswagen (VW) special with the engine, mildly tuned and with larger valves, turned around through 180 degrees. This mid-engined layout was inherited from the Auto-Union racers via the pre-war Project 114 sports car.

The body was wide at the front to enable spats to be fitted over the front wheels, and tapered towards the back of the car. The body sides were flat, with a straight-through wing line. Both the front and rear ends fell away in graceful curves, allowing VW headlamps to be fitted.

The windscreen consisted of two frameless flat panes, meeting in a V and supported only by a central pillar. The seat was of the bench type, with a shaped backrest giving some lateral support. The simple dashboard, dominated by a large speedometer, was positioned directly in front of the driver. The body was handbeaten from aluminium sheets, which became a characteristic of Gmünd-built cars.

The first Porsche received its road-worthiness certificate on 8 June 1948.

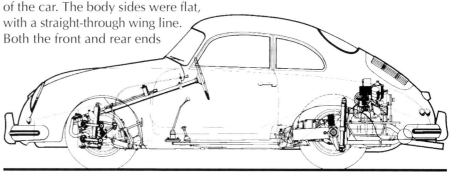

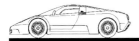

ASTON MARTIN DB2

Country of origin: UK
Date: 1950
Engine: dohc inline 4-cylinder with 12 overhead valves producing 79.8kW (107bhp) at 5,000rpm
Transmission: 4-speed manual
Wheels driven: rear
Capacity: 2,580cc (157.4cu in)
Bore & stroke: 78 x 90mm (3.1 x 3.5in)
Performance: maximum speed 170.6km/h (106mph); 0–96.5km/h (60mph) in 12.7 seconds; 0–402m (0.25 mile) in 18.7 seconds
Dimensions: wheelbase 2.515m (8ft 3in); length 4.102m (13ft 5.5in); width 1.651m (5ft 5in); height 1.359m (4ft 5.5in); track 1.372m (4ft 6in) front, 1.372m (4ft 4.8in) rear
Kerb weight: 1,135kg (2,500lb)
Fuel: 86.4l (19.0gal/22.8US gal)
Suspension: independent coil springs front and rear
Brakes: front discs, rear drums
Compression ratio: 6.5 : 1

Aston Martin has been building cars since 1922 and although its financial basis was not always its strongest point, the superb quality of its sports cars has never been in question. The company was bought by David Brown, who later acquired Lagonda, in 1947.

Post-war production began with the DB1. Although at the time it was launched as a 1,950cc (126cu in) sports model and despite only 15 examples being built, its tubular chassis laid the foundation for the DB2.

The acquisition of Lagonda provided Aston Martin with the power unit it needed, a twin-cam engine designed by W.O. Bentley; the DB1 had been distinctly underpowered. The result was a winner, a road car with style and elegance that more than held its own in endurance races. It came fifth at Le Mans in 1950, when it shared the Index. The DB2 later took 1–2–3 in class in the Tourist Trophy and won its class in the 1952 and 1953 Mille Miglias.

Production totalled 410 units before the model was replaced by the DB2/4, which retained the DB2 engine. The DB2/4 Mk II followed in 1956, and the Mk III in 1957.

Below: *a 1952 DB2 drophead coupé*

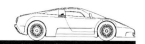

MG TD

Country of origin: UK
Date: 1950
Engine: inline 4-cylinder with overhead valves and twin 38mm (1.5in) SU carburettors, producing 40.6kW (54.4bhp) at 5,200rpm
Transmission: 4-speed manual
Wheels driven: rear
Capacity: 1,250cc (76.3cu in)
Bore & stroke: 66.5 x 90mm (2.6 x 3.5in)
Performance: maximum speed 127km/h (78.9mph); 0–96.5km/h (60mph) in 19.4 seconds
Dimensions: wheelbase 2.388m (7ft 10in); length 3.658m (12ft); width 1.488m (4ft 10.6in); height 1.344m (4ft 4.9in); track 1.204m (3ft 11.4in) front and 1.27m (4ft 2in) rear
Steering: rack and pinion
Kerb weight: 910.3kg (2,005lb)
Suspension: independent coil and wishbone front; non-independent semi-elliptic leaf springs with dampers at rear
Brakes: drums front and rear
Compression ratio: 7.25 : 1

Following the success of the TC in North America, some 90 per cent of the near-30,000 TD units built had left-hand drive. Improved suspension and smaller and wider wheels both added to the improved road holding of the TD. However, speed was still lacking although factory tuning kits produced 67.1kW (90bhp), and the bigger engine introduced in 1954 provided 47kW (63bhp).

The TD was the first MG since the mid-1930s to incorporate major styling changes. The TD was easily recognisible as the descendant of the TC although every panel

was different, but it retained the vertical slat radiator, flowing front wings and running boards. Still the bonnet was centrally hinged, the spare wheel carried at the rear, and there were no direction indicators as standard.

Another innovation on the TD was the fitting of sturdy chromium-plated bumpers and over-riders at both front and rear, and the replacement of the TC's traditional wire spoke wheels with pressed-steel disc wheels. This was a result of having to accommodate the arms and links of the new rack and pinion steering.

JAGUAR C-TYPE

Country of origin: UK
Date: 1951
Engine: dohc inline 6-cylinder with twin carburettors, producing 149.1kW (200bhp) at 5,800rpm
Transmission: 4-speed manual
Wheels driven: rear
Capacity: 3,442cc (210cu in)
Bore & stroke: 83 x 116mm (3.3 x 4.2in)
Performance: maximum speed 243km/h (151mph); 0–96.5km/h (60mph) in 6.6 seconds
Dimensions: wheelbase 2.438m (8ft); length 3.988m (13ft 1in); width 1.638m (5ft 4.5in); height 1.08m (3ft 6.5in); track 1.295m (4ft 3in) front and rear
Steering: rack and pinion
Kerb weight: 1,017kg (2,240lb)
Fuel: 189.2l (41.6gal/50US gal)
Suspension: double wishbone and torsion bars front; twin trailing arms, torsion bars and Panhard rod at rear
Brakes: drums front and rear
Compression ratio: 8 : 1

The year 1951 marked the beginning of the Jaguar legend. The outstanding reception awarded to the XK120 and its sporting successes notwithstanding, it was the emergence of the Mark VII saloon which put Jaguar on top of the commercially more important saloon market. In motor sport it was the company's decision to build a true racing car as a contender for Le Mans which finally and irrevocably put the Jaguar name on the roll of honour.

The C-Type was basically an XK120 with a spaceframe for a chassis and a specially-tuned engine, developing 149.1kW (200bhp). It provided Jaguar with wins at Le Mans in 1951 and 1953, on the later occasion using Dunlop disc brakes which gave it a distinct advantage over the other competitors. The C was a classic shape; there were just 53 built between 1951 and 1953, and the first three built – at the time, the only three in existence – all took part in the 1951 Le Mans race. Two, including one driven by Stirling Moss and Jack Fairman, which had broken the lap record and was leading at the time, were forced to retire; the third car, driven by Peter Walker and Peter Whitehead, went on to win at a record average speed of more than 150km/h (93mph).

Bottom: *a C-Type at Le Mans in 1953, the high point of the car's career*

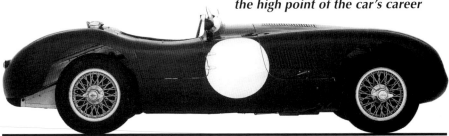

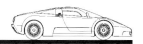

FERRARI 340 America

Country of origin: Italy
Date: 1951
Engine: 'long block' 60-degree sohc V12 with triple Weber 1F/4C or 42DCZ carburettors, producing 238.5kW (320bhp) at 7,000rpm
Transmission: 4-speed manual, all-synchromesh
Wheels driven: rear
Capacity: 4,494cc (274.1cu in)
Bore & stroke: 80 x 74mm (3.2 x 2.98in)
Performance: maximum speed 289.6km/h (180mph); 0–161km/h (100mph) in 11.5 seconds
Dimensions: wheelbase 2.6m (8ft 8in); track 1.325m (4ft 5in) front, 1.32m (4ft 4.8in) rear
Steering: worm and sector
Suspension: independent; double wishbones and transverse leaf springs front; live axle, semi-elliptic leaf springs and trailing arms at rear
Brakes: hydraulic aluminium drums front and rear; iron liners
Compression ratio: 9 : 1

Above: *the specification for the 375 MM sports racing version;* right, *the 410 with fins, and* below, *a later 410 powered by a 4.9-litre engine*

The 340 America was built in a number of sport and GT versions, all using a similar engine, originally derived from a Ferrari Formula One car. None of the 22 built was identical with any other.

The 342 America followed in 1952, and was one step up from the 340 in terms of finish. It utilised the same basic engine, but was strictly a street car, with the power reduced from 207 to 170kW (280 to 230bhp).

Ferrari launched the first of its big-engined sports cars in the following year. The 375 America was intended to complement the 250 Export and Europa models. Like the 340 and 342 models, the 375 was built in small numbers and often produced as a one-off for an individual client. The engines were 4,522cc (276cu in) V12s inclined at 60 degrees, and produced 222kW (300bhp).

The 410 Superamerica replaced the 375 in 1956, using a 4,963cc (303cu in) 60-degree V12 engine which produced 252kW (340bhp), and was also derived from a Formula One car. The model underwent continuous development in order to increase performance and refine styling. The original 1956 version sported sedate tail fins; post-1957 Superfast models had shorter wheelbases reduced from 2.79 to 2.59m (110 to 102in), and by the time the third and final series appeared in 1958 the engine power had been raised to 296kW (400bhp).

The 400 Superamerica was the last in the series, appearing in 1961 with the 3,967cc (242cu in) 296kW (400bhp) 60-degree V12. Only a few examples were produced, but both hardtop and cabriolet versions were available.

MORGAN PLUS FOUR

Country of origin: UK
Date: 1952
Engine: Standard Vanguard inline
4-cylinder ohv, producing 50.7kW
(68bhp) at 4,200rpm
Transmission: 4-speed manual
Wheels driven: rear
Capacity: 2,088cc (127.4cu in)
Bore & stroke: 85.1 x 91.9mm (3.3 x
3.6in)
Performance: maximum speed
138km/h (86mph); 0–96.5km/h
(60mph) in 17.9 seconds
Dimensions: wheelbase 2.438m (8ft);
length 3.556m (11ft 8in); width
1.422m (4ft 8in); height 1.321m (4ft
4in); track 1.194m (3ft 11in) front
and rear
Steering: worm and roller
Kerb weight: 853kg (1,880lb)
Fuel: 50l (11gal/13.2US gal)
Suspension: coil springs front; leaf
springs rear
Brakes: drums front and rear
Compression ratio: 6.7 : 1

Founded in 1910, Morgan made only three-wheelers until 1936, but the 4/4 model made from that year was intrinsically the same car as is made today. Morgan resumed production after the War with the 4/4, replacing it with the Plus Four in 1951, a Standard Vanguard-engined version.

The Plus Four had a 101mm (four-inch) larger wheelbase, in order to accommodate the 2,088cc (127.4cu in) engine which was driven through a Moss gearbox similar to that used on the Jaguar XK120. Its performance was not startling, but it was better than the very popular MG TD. Like its predecessor, the Plus Four had a separate steel chassis, topped by a choice of traditional-looking roadster bodies erected from steel panels over a wooden frame.

Morgan introduced a revised body style in 1953, which had a curved radiator grille, extended front wings and the headlight units flared into the body. Production lasted until 1955 with only 245 being built, partly because of the restrictions on the Vanguard engine. However, it was phased out while the new Plus Four was being phased in from 1954.

It had the Triumph TR2 engine of 1,991cc (121.5cu in), yielding 67.1kW (90bhp) which transformed the Plus Four. During the 15 years which followed, Morgan produced 3,390 units incorporating later TR series engines, and by the time the Plus Four was retired in 1969, its top speed was over 170km/h (105mph).

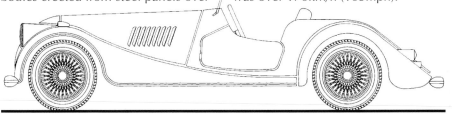

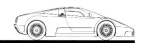

AUSTIN-HEALEY 100M

Country of origin: UK
Date: 1953
Engine: inline 4-cylinder ohv,
producing 67.1kW (90bhp) at 4,000rpm
Transmission: 5-speed with overdrive
Wheels driven: rear
Capacity: 2,660cc (162.3cu in)
Bore & stroke: 87.3 x 111.1mm (3.4
x 4.4in)
Performance: maximum speed
191.5km/h (119mph); 0–96.5km/h
(60mph) in 10.3 seconds
Dimensions: wheelbase 2.286m (7ft
6in); length 3.848m (12ft 7.5in); width
1.537m (5ft 0.5in); height 1.245m
(4ft 1in); track 1.237m (4ft 0.7in)
front and 1.288m (4ft 2.7in) rear
Steering: cam & peg
Kerb weight: 953.4kg (2,100lb)
Fuel: 54.6l (12gal/14.4US gal)
Suspension: independent double wish-
bones and coil springs front; live axle
with semi-elliptic leaf springs at rear
Brakes: hydraulic drums front and rear
Compression ratio: 7.5 : 1

Founded as the Donald Healey Motor Company, the factory built a two-seater model from Austin components in 1952. The car was tested in Belgium, where it recorded a speed of 188km/h (117mph). On returning to London, it became the star of the Earls Court Motor Show. There it was seen by the managing director of the British Motor Corporation (BMC), Sir Leonard Lord, who promptly bought the company.

The individual and beautiful Austin-Healey 100 was therefore not built in a limited quantity but mass-produced in tens of thousands by one of Britain's biggest manufacturers.

The 100 was appealing, sturdy and simple; its power block was the 2.7l (162cu in) all-iron 4-cylinder from the Austin A90, which produced

67.1kW (90bhp) at 4,000rpm. It had centre-lock wire wheels as standard, and a three-position windscreen which could be folded down flat.

The performance and handling were excellent, and were matched by only a few cars of similar price. Production of the model lasted only three and a half years but spanned many variants, including the original BN1, of which 10,633 units were built; the BN2, introduced in 1955 and which ran to 2,765 units; and the 100M, of which 1,159 were built. This variant of the BN2 offered 82kW (110bhp) at 4,500rpm, two-tone paint and some detail modifications.

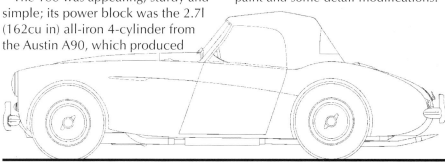

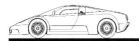

CHEVROLET CORVETTE

Country of origin: USA
Date: 1953
Engine: V8 ohv with a single 4-barrel carburettor, producing 167.8kW (225bhp) at 5,200rpm
Transmission: close-ratio 3-speed manual
Wheels driven: rear
Capacity: 4,344cc (265cu in)
Bore & stroke: 95.3 x 76.2mm (3.8 x 3in)
Performance: maximum speed 207.7km/h (129.1mph); 0–96.5km/h (60mph) in 7.3 seconds
Dimensions: wheelbase 2.591m (8ft 6in); length 4.267m (14ft); width 1.791m (5ft 10.5in); height 1.298m (4ft 3.1in); track 1.44m (4ft 8.7in) front, 1.494m (4ft 10.8in) rear
Steering: recirculating ball
Kerb weight: 1,352kg (2,980lb)
Suspension: unequal-length A-arms, coil springs, tubular shock absorbers and anti-roll bar front; live axle on semi-elliptic leaf springs with tubular shock absorbers at rear
Brakes: hydraulic; drums front and rear
Compression ratio: 9.3 : 1

This specification refers to the 1956 model

Chevrolet had been founded in 1911, and prior to the Corvette's launch the company had built its reputation on selling value for money cars. It had joined General Motors (GM) in 1917, and by 1931 had become America's most popular make.

Competition between Chevrolet and Ford was as fierce as ever during the 1950s, when America was consumed by fins and chrome but also fascinated by the small British sports cars. Harley Earl, GM's head of styling, suggested the production of a low-priced 111.9kW (150bhp) sports car in 1951, and the result was the launch of the Corvette in 1953.

The original 'Vette sold just under 4,000 units but was bedevilled by teething troubles during the 1950s and almost never saw the light of day. When it did, it became the first-ever mass-produced fibreglass-bodied sports car.

Ed Cole's new 4.3-litre (265cu in) engine replaced the original 3.8-litre (234cu in) straight six in 1955. The power went up, the top speed went up, and the Corvette had been saved. It emerged as a new car in 1956, with a newly styled body. By 1958, the Corvette was selling at about 10,000 units per year.

Below: an original 1953 model Corvette

Above: a 1961 model which had a 170kW (230bhp) V8 engine

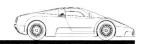

FERRARI 250GT

Country of origin: Italy
Date: 1954
Engine: V12 ohv with triple carburettors, producing 179kW (240bhp) at 7,000rpm
Transmission: 4-speed manual
Wheels driven: rear
Capacity: 2,953cc (180.2cu in)
Bore & stroke: 72.9 x 58.7mm (2.9 x 2.3in)
Performance: maximum speed 202.7km/h (126mph); 0–96.5km/h (60mph) in 7.1 seconds
Dimensions: wheelbase 2.601m (8ft 6.4in); length 4.394m (14ft 5in); width 1.651m (5ft 5in); height 1.397m (4ft 7in); track 1.354m (4ft 5.3in) front, 1.349m (4ft 5.1in) rear
Steering: worm and sector
Kerb weight: 1,225kg (2,700lb)
Fuel: 99.9l (22gal/26.4US gal)
Suspension: coil springs and frame tubes front; leaf springs rear
Brakes: drums front and rear
Compression ratio: 9.2 : 1

Until the 250 Europa of 1953, production Ferraris had been competition cars with detuned engines and road-style bodies. The 250 Europa was designed specifically for road use, with a long wheelbase.

Ferrari made the huge step towards becoming a volume producer the following year, with the launch of the 250GT. It built 902 units between 1954 and 1962, whereas previously only the 212 Inter model of 1950–1 had exceeded 50 units.

The 250GT became known as the 'long wheelbase' although it was still 203mm (8in) shorter than the Europa. Ferrari launched the so-called 'short' wheelbase, the 250GT SWB, at 2.4m (7ft 10.5in) in 1959. It was designed by Giovanni Battista 'Pinin'Farina as a Berlinetta, and is said to have been his favourite car. Now regarded as the most perfect encapsulation of the Ferrari ethos, it was better, tighter, lighter, faster and prettier than the 250GT. It had a blunter face, open headlights and a glassier cockpit that created the impression of a more practical car; it was both clean and balanced, truly a masterpiece.

This specification refers to the 250GT Cabriolet, 1958; below, a 250GT SWB; bottom, the 250GT Tour de France

JAGUAR XK140

Country of origin: UK
Date: 1954
Engine: dohc inline 6-cylinder with twin carburettors, producing 141.7kW (190bhp) at 5,750rpm
Transmission: 4-speed manual
Wheels driven: rear
Capacity: 3,442cc (210cu in)
Bore & stroke: 83 x 106mm (3.3 x 4.2in)
Performance: maximum speed 210km/h (130mph); 0–96.5km/h (60mph) in 8.4 seconds
Dimensions: wheelbase 2.591m (8ft 8in); length 4.47m (14ft 8in); width 1.638m (5ft 4.5in); height 1.358m (4ft 5.5in); track 1.308m (4ft 3.5in) front, 1.305m (4ft 3.4in)
Steering: rack and pinion
Kerb weight: 1,345kg (2,965lb)
Fuel: 63.7l (14gal/16.8US gal)
Suspension: independent torsion bars front; semi-elliptic springs rear
Brakes: Lockheed hydraulic drums front and rear
Compression ratio: 8 : 1

Replacing the XK120 was no easy task; so advanced and successful had the model been that it gave the company a base from which it was able to enter motor sports with the C-Type and D-Type models. The XK140 was an updated XK120 that from the start was available as a roadster, a coupé and a drophead coupé.

The XK140 retained the 120's heavy box-section chassis and the same suspension; it even retained the twin-cam six engine, but its power was increased from 134.2kW (180bhp) to 141.7kW (190bhp). Externally

the XK140 was distinguishable by heftier bumpers and fewer grille bars, and the cockpit afforded more room, as the engine had been sited 76.2mm (3in) farther forward.

As a whole, the 140 was heavier but more comfortable and easier to handle. The new model offered excellent value for money at only £100 ($280) more than the 120 and sales continued on a high with 8,884 units being produced before being replaced by the XK150 in 1957.

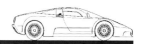

MERCEDES-BENZ 300SL COUPÉ

Country of origin: Germany
Date: 1954
Engine: sohc inline 6-cylinder with fuel injection, producing 179kW (240bhp) at 6,100rpm
Transmission: 4-speed manual
Wheels driven: rear
Capacity: 2,996cc (182.8cu in)
Bore & stroke: 85 x 88mm (3.3 x 3.5in)
Performance: maximum speed 217.2km/h (135mph); 0–96.5km/h (60mph) in 8.8 seconds
Dimensions: wheelbase 2.388m (7ft 10in); length 4.445m (14ft 7in); width 1.778m (5ft 10in); height 1.295m (4ft 3in); track 1.384m (4ft 6.5in) front, 1.435m (4ft 8.5in) rear
Kerb weight: 1,252kg (2,758lb)
Fuel: 127.4l (28gal/33.6US gal)
Suspension: upper and lower A-arms, coil springs, and anti-roll bar front; high-pivot swing axles on radius arms, coil springs at rear
Brakes: hydraulic front, drums rear
Compression ratio: 8.5 : 1

The famed Gullwing, conceived as a sports racer, proved its credentials long before the production model appeared. Ten SL prototypes were produced in 1952.

Full-height, side-opening doors would have compromised rigidity in this high-sided structure, and so half-doors were developed for the coupés that were hinged at the roof centre to lift upwards; hence the now famous gullwing design.

The 300SL (Sport Light) was an instant success on the racetrack, finishing second and fourth in the 1952 Mille Miglia and winning that year's Le Mans 24-Hour race outright. That success prompted an order for 1,000 units from the American

importer, Max Hoffmann, and the SL coupé was unveiled at the 1954 New York motor show.

The production run lasted until 1957, when the coupé was replaced by the roadster which had a space-frame re-designed for conventional doors. Both the coupé and the roadster, for which a factory hard top was listed, were strictly two-seaters. Both sported the typical Mercedes dashboard, with plenty of chrome and dominated by high-set speedometers and tachometers.

Manufacture of the roadster ceased in 1963 after a production run of 1,858 units; this was 458 more than for its sibling coupé.

ALFA ROMEO GUILIETTA SS

Country of origin: Italy
Date: 1955
Engine: dohc inline 4-cylinder, producing 59.7kW (80bhp) at 6,000rpm
Transmission: 4-speed manual
Wheels driven: rear
Capacity: 1,290cc (78.7cu in)
Bore & stroke: 73.9 x 74.9mm (2.91 x 2.95in)
Performance: maximum speed 165.7km/h (103mph); 0–96.5km/h (60mph) in 13.2 seconds
Dimensions: wheelbase 2.38m (7ft 9.7in); length 3.98m (13ft 0.7in); width 1.534m (5ft 0.4in); height 1.318m (4ft 3.9in); track 1.285m (4ft 2.6in) front, 1.27m (4ft 2in) rear
Steering: worm and roller
Kerb weight: 948.9kg (2,090lb)
Fuel: 40.0l (8.8gal/10.6US gal)
Suspension: coil springs front and rear
Brakes: drums front and rear
Compression ratio: 8.5 : 1

Alfa introduced its first mass-produced model in 1950. The 1900 was a four-door saloon with a monocoque chassis, an 1,884cc (114.9cu in) engine and a top speed of 161km/h (100mph). In 1954, a 1900 Sprint was introduced with the same engine but with a choice of coupé (designed by Touring) or cabriolet (by Pininfarina) bodies, together with a Super Sprint. The latter was powered by a 85kW (115bhp) 1,975cc (120.5cu in) dohc engine, which provided a top speed of 177km/h (110mph).

The two-seater Guilietta Sprint coupé was introduced in 1955, together with a Sprint Veloce.

The Sprint had a 59.7kW (80bhp) and the Veloce a 67.1kW (90bhp) engine. There were also a Guilietta Spyder and Spyder Veloce, an open version, which was introduced at the same time. The Spyder versions had a floor gearchange, the Sprint Veloce initially having a part-alloy body and sliding Perspex windows.

Production of all versions ended in 1962. There was also an SS version from 1957–62, which was regarded as the ultimate model styled by Bertone, with engine output at 74.6kW (100bhp) and a maximum speed increased to over 194km/h (120mph).

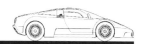

FORD THUNDERBIRD

Country of origin: USA
Date: 1955
Engine: V8 ohv, single Holley carburettor, producing 147.6kW (198bhp) at 4,400rpm
Transmission: 3-speed manual
Wheels driven: rear
Capacity: 4,788cc (292.1cu in)
Bore & stroke: 95.3 x 83.8mm (3.8 x 3.3in)
Performance: maximum speed 177.2km/h (110.1mph); 0–96.5km/h (60mph) in 9.5 seconds
Dimensions: wheelbase 2.591m (8ft 6in); length 4.699m (15ft 5in); width 1.783m (5ft 10in); height 1.326m (4ft 4in); track 1.422m (4ft 8in) front and rear
Kerb weight: 1,471kg (3,240lb)
Fuel: 61.9l (13.6gal/16.3US gal)
Suspension: independent A-arms, coil springs, ball joints, link stabiliser bar and tubular shock absorbers front; rigid axle, longitudinal leaf springs and tubular shock absorbers rear
Brakes: drums front and rear
Compression ratio: 8.5 : 1

The launch of the Corvette in 1953 certainly threw many manufacturers into hair-tearing desperation. However, Ford predicated a fibreglass-bodied two-seater and set about designing a Corvette fighter, producing what it termed a personal car. This was intended to introduce a thrill to routine driving but was never conceived by Ford as a money-spinner, with sales predictions pitched at 10,000 units per year.

The two-seater 'little' Thunderbird was meant to enhance Ford's image. Sales were better than expected, as the price was not really competitive and buyers were also selecting from a whole range of optional extras.

The mid-1950s in America were a power race; in 1956 the base engine output was raised to 150.6kW (202bhp), while at the top end a 193.9kW (260bhp) 5,114cc (312cu in) unit was available. The following year, base engine output was raised a further 7.45kW (10bhp), thanks mainly to an increased compression ratio of 9.1 : 1. At the top of the power range was a new supercharged F series engine modified with reinforced cylinder heads, special combustion chambers with lower compression ratios, a dual-point distributor, a hotter camshaft and a special fuel pump. Its official rating of 223.7kW (300bhp) was more likely nearer to 253.5kW (340bhp).

Unfortunately, Ford was right: the 'little' two-seater Thunderbird with its sturdy steel body and convenient roll-up windows did not make economic sense. It was discontinued in 1957, making way for the big-engined four-seater 'Squarebird' on its production line.

Above: *the 1955 convertible coupe*

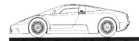

MERCEDES-BENZ 190SL

Country of origin: Germany
Date: 1955
Engine: sohc inline 4-cylinder, producing 89.5kW (120bhp) at 5,700rpm
Transmission: 4-speed manual
Wheels driven: rear
Capacity: 1,897cc (115.7cu in)
Bore & stroke: 85.1 x 83.6mm (3.35 x 3.3in)
Performance: maximum speed 160.6km/h (99.8mph); 0–96.5km/h (60mph) in 13 seconds
Dimensions: wheelbase 2.4m (7ft 10.5in); length 4.293m (14ft 1in); width 1.740m (5ft 8.5in); height 1.321m (4ft 4in); track 1.430m (4ft 8.3in) front, 1.481m (4ft 10.3in) rear
Steering: not known
Kerb weight: 1,135kg (2,500lb)
Fuel: 65.1l (14.3gal/17.2US gal)
Suspension: coil springs and double wishbone front; swing axle rear
Brakes: drums front and rear
Compression ratio: 8.5 : 1

The 190SL was bred from the W120 series 180 saloon, and indeed was originally coded W121. It used an abbreviated version of the 180's platform, to which was welded the roadster bodyshell. The 180's suspension was also retained, but power came from a new overhead cam four-cylinder, initially with twin Solex carburettors. The car's heavy weight kept its top speed down to about 161km/h (100mph).

Like many another 1950s Mercedes, the 190 had a wide mouth grille which bore the three-pointed star, a long nose and wheelarch

eyebrows. A hard-top version was later added to the line up, together with a fixed-top coupé.

The 190SL remained in production until 1963, and sold a total of well over 25,000 units. There were few alterations during its lifetime, although the coupé had a larger rear window.

Regarded as the little brother of the 300SL, it was often unfortunately and unfavourably compared to it. It was a strikingly good-looking car, with the manner and looks of a sports car but not top performance. It was often considered an ideal sporting vehicle for women.

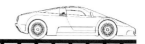

MGA

Country of origin: UK
Date: 1955
Engine: water-cooled ohv inline 4-cylinder with twin SU carburettors, producing 50.7kW (68bhp) at 5,500rpm
Transmission: 4-speed manual
Wheels driven: rear
Capacity: 1,488cc (90.8cu in)
Bore & stroke: 73 x 88.9mm (2.9 x 3.5in)
Performance: maximum speed 153km/h (95.1mph); 0–96.5km/h (60mph) in 14.5 seconds
Dimensions: wheelbase 2.388m (7ft 10in); length 3.962m (13ft); width 1.473m (4ft 10in); height 1.27m (4ft 2in); track 1.204m (3ft 11.4in) front and 1.24m (4ft 0.8in) rear
Kerb weight: 917.1kg (2,020lb)
Fuel: 45.5l (10gal/12US gal)
Suspension: coil springs, wishbones and lever arm dampers front; live axle, half-elliptic leaf springs and lever arm dampers at rear
Brakes: 254mm (10in) drums all round
Compression ratio: 8.3 : 1

The prototype car was finished in 1952, but not introduced until the life expectancy of the TFs, descendants of the TC and the TD, had been realised. Thus the MGA was introduced in 1955. In its first full production year of 1956 a staggering 13,000 units were built, far exceeding expectations. MG had evidently launched the right car at the right time.

The A had a rigid chassis, coupled with modern styling and a twin-carb version of the BMC series B engine. In the coupé version, introduced in 1956, this produced 53.7kW (72bhp) at 5,500rpm.

The front suspension system was directly related to that of the TF, while the rear suspension was derived from the ZA Magnette.

Total production of the MGA and A coupé versions reached 58,750 units. The A twin-cam introduced in 1958 sold 2,111 and the MGA 1600 with the 1,588cc (96.9cu in) 59.7kW (80bhp) engine, which replaced the A and A coupé versions in 1959, had sales of 31,601. The final Mk II version, which was produced between 1961 and 1962 and which brought the top speed to over the important 161km/h (100mph) mark sold 8,719 units. This brought sales of MGAs in all versions to over 100,000 units, and as before a high percentage of these found their way across the Atlantic.

TRIUMPH TR3

Country of origin: UK
Date: 1955
Engine: inline 4-cylinder ohv, producing 70.8kW (95bhp) at 4,800rpm
Transmission: 4-speed manual; overdrive optional
Wheels driven: rear
Capacity: 1,991cc (121.5cu in)
Bore & stroke: 83.1 x 91.9mm (3.3 x 3.6in)
Performance: maximum speed 168.5km/h (104.7mph); 0–96.5km/h (60mph) in 12 seconds
Dimensions: wheelbase 2.235m (7ft 4in); length 3.835m (12ft 7in); width 1.41m (4ft 7.5in); height 1.27m (4ft 2in); track 1.143m (3ft 11in) front, 1.156m (3ft 9.5in) rear
Kerb weight: 949kg (2,090lb)
Suspension: upper and lower A-arms and coil springs front; live axle, semi-elliptic leaf springs rear
Brakes: drums front and rear
Compression ratio: 8.5 : 1

As sales of the TR2 slowed down in 1954, production began to run ahead of demand and the Standard Triumph company was forced to stockpile. Undaunted, it pressed ahead with the development of the TR2's replacement, and launched the TR3 in 1955. This was much improved, outwardly distinguishable by a grille, filling the TR2's recessed mouth.

The TR3 became the first British series-built car with standard front disc brakes in 1956. As for the TR2, a factory hard top was available from 1954, as part of a GT option.

The TR3's power was increased by 3.7kW (5bhp) over that of the TR2, but because it was also 63.5kg (140lb) heavier, the extra power did nothing to increase its performance – and indeed, many complained that fuel efficiency suffered. The TR2 had sold 8,628 units between 1953–5, but the TR3 did better, selling 13,378 between 1956–7, when it made way for the TR3A, an interim model which

Above *and* below: *the wider-grilled TR3A*

became a bestseller, and with the TR3B topped sales of 60,000 units before the TR4 came along.

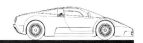

BMW 507

Country of origin: Germany
Date: 1956
Engine: aluminium V8 ohv with 2 valves per cylinder and 2 Zenith carburettors, producing 115.6kW (155bhp) at 5,000rpm
Transmission: 4-speed manual
Wheels driven: rear
Capacity: 3,168cc (193.3cu in)
Bore & stroke: 82 x 74.9mm (3.2 x 2.9in)
Performance: maximum speed 199.5km/h (124mph); 0–96.5km/h (60mph) in 8.8 seconds
Dimensions: wheelbase 2.479m (8ft 1.6in); track 1.44m (4ft 8.7in) front, 1.42m (4ft 7.9in) rear
Kerb weight: 1,307kg (2,880lb)
Suspension: unequal-length independent wishbones, torsion bars and anti-roll bar front; live axle, radius rods, A-bracket and torsion bars rear
Brakes: hydraulic front, drums at rear
Compression ratio: 7.8 : 1

Launched in 1955, BMW's first post-war sporting coupé and cabriolet model was based on the pre-war 6-cylinder 327 and 328 sports cars. It followed the 501 and 502 saloons, and thus logically was designated the 503. However, it proved to be a trifle ponderous, and although it remained in production until 1960, sales reached only 412 units.

The decidedly unexciting 503 fixed-head coupé was designed by Albrecht Goertz. It is surprising then to consider that in addition he was responsible for the stunningly styled 507. This model was a real beauty and entered production in 1956 but was withdrawn in 1959, after only

252 had been produced. The 507 is heavy but handles well and looks superb in both roadster and hardtop coupé versions, being long and low, with a pointed nose and twin grille reminiscent of the classic early BMWs. Thin in section, this is one of the smoothest, classiest car bodies ever; unfortunately, as with many classics, its undoing was its price tag.

The 507 was offered with a higher rear-axle ratio, which allowed a maximum speed of 217km/h (135mph). The gear change was on the floor, and front disc brakes were fitted on some later models.

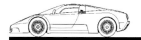

JAGUAR XK150

Country of origin: UK
Date: 1957
Engine: dohc inline 6-cylinder with twin carburettors, producing 156.6kW (210bhp) at 5,500rpm
Transmission: 4-speed manual
Wheels driven: rear
Capacity: 3,442cc (210cu in)
Bore & stroke: 83.1 x 105.9mm (3.3 x 4.2in)
Performance: maximum speed 195.7km/h (121.6mph); 0–96.5km/h (60mph) in 9.5 seconds
Dimensions: wheelbase 2.591m (8ft 6in); length 4.496m (14ft 9in); width 1.638m (5ft 4.5in); height 1.397m (4ft 7in); track 1.311m (4ft 3.6in) front and rear
Steering: rack and pinion
Kerb weight: 1,402kg (3,090lb)
Fuel: 63.7l (14gal/16.8US gal)
Suspension: independent torsion bars front; semi-elliptic springs rear
Brakes: Dunlop discs front and rear
Compression ratio: 8 : 1

The XK150 carried on where the XK140 had left off. It looked good and was a high-performing and value-for-money sports car that sold well. The 150 was certainly the most developed of the series, though perhaps it was being refined away from its true sporting heritage.

A changing market hastened the introduction of the 150 in 1957, which was Jaguar's reply to the introduction of German rivals in the form of BMW's 507 and Mercedes' 300SL, both offering comparable performance but being aimed more specifically at the North American market, where comfort was much more of a purchasing decision factor.

The 150 was thus more civilised than the 140; the bodyshell, extensively restyled, introduced higher front bumpers and a recontoured body line. There was a wider grille, and a one-piece windscreen; that of the 140 had been a split V-type. Also new for the 150 were servo-assisted Dunlop disc brakes, a feature tried successfully by Jaguar on its racing D-Types.

Initially the 150 was offered as a coupé or convertible, with the roadster following nine months into production. The 3,781cc (230.7cu in) engine was introduced in 1959, and the XK150 finally bowed out in 1961 to make way for the E-Type.

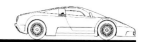

ASTON MARTIN DB4

Country of origin: UK
Date: 1958
Engine: aluminium dohc inline 6-cylinder with twin SU carburettors, producing 196.1kW (263bhp) at 5,700rpm
Transmission: 4-speed manual
Wheels driven: rear
Capacity: 3,760cc (223.9cu in)
Bore & stroke: 91.9 x 91.9mm (3.6 x 3.6in)
Performance: maximum speed 225.6km/h (140.2mph); 0–96.5km/h (60mph) in 7.5 seconds
Dimensions: wheelbase 2.489m (8ft 2in); length 4.496m (14ft 9in); width 1.676m (5ft 6in); height 1.321m (4ft 4in); track 1.372m (4ft 6in) front, 1.359m (4ft 5.5in) rear
Kerb weight: 1,309kg (2,884lb)
Suspension: independent coil springs and unequal wishbones front; rigid axle, coil springs and parallel trailing links rear
Brakes: 4-wheel hydraulics, Dunlop discs front and rear
Compression ratio: 8.3 : 1

Aston Martin set about replacing the ageing DB2 in 1955. Although the company had the option of a completely fresh design, and of creating the first entirely new Aston Martin road car since David Brown had acquired the company, the resultant DB4 was evolutionary rather than revolutionary. It was unmistakeably an Aston Martin.

The complicated dohc six-cylinder engine was another Tom Marek design which proved expensive to build as well as being heavy. That aside, it provided ferocious power for the new model and a real 0–161–0km/h (100mph) time of a breathtaking 27 seconds, straight off the showroom floor; in consequence it had no competition.

Carrozzeria Touring of Milan provided the body style, and its *superleggera* style of construction, with aluminium panels on a thin tubular steel framework.

A convertible was added to the range in 1961. By the time that production ceased in 1963, 1,103 units had been produced. A further 75 DB4GTs were produced between 1960 and 1963. These were DB4 Vantage variants, each having a 127mm (5in) shorter wheelbase and lower roof line. The car widely considered to be the ultimate DB4 was the DB4GT Zagato, which was capable of reaching 0–96.5km/h (60mph) in 6.1 seconds, and was built between 1961 and 1963.

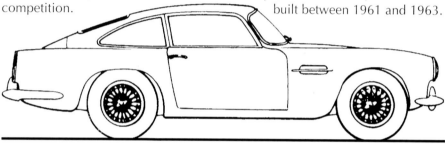

AUSTIN-HEALEY 3000 MKI

Country of origin: UK
Date: 1959
Engine: inline 6-cylinder ohv, producing 92.5kW (124bhp) at 4,600rpm
Transmission: 4-speed manual with overdrive on 3 and 4
Wheels driven: rear
Capacity: 2,912cc (177.7cu in)
Bore & stroke: 83.3 x 88.9mm (3.3 x 3.5in)
Performance: maximum speed 186.6km/h (116mph); 0–96.5km/h (60mph) in 11.4 seconds
Dimensions: wheelbase 2.337m (7ft 8in); length 4.001m (13ft 1.5in); width 1.537m (5ft 0.5in); height 1.27m (4ft 2in); track 1.237m (4ft 0.7in) front, 1.27m (4ft 2in) rear
Steering: cam and peg
Kerb weight: 1,140kg (2,513lb)
Fuel: 54.6l (12gal/14.4US gal)
Suspension: coil springs front; leaf springs rear
Brakes: discs front, drums rear
Compression ratio: 9 : 1

The 3000 replaced the 100/6 in 1959, and as the name suggests, this version had a 3-litre engine. In order to cope with this, it also had front disc brakes. The Mark I, of which 13,650 units were sold, gave way to the Mk II in 1961, of which 5,450 units were sold. This had a new gearbox and triple SU carburettors, which raised the output to 98.4kW (132bhp). The new gearbox had a more directly-acting selector mechanism.

At the end of 1962, the Mk II received a superficial facelift, and was renamed the Mk II convertible. Its general appearance did not change, but there were roll-up windows, a more curved windscreen and a proper fold-away soft top. The engine reverted to twin SUs, and the two-seater option was dropped; all 3000s were now 2+2s.

In the Spring of 1964 the 3000 underwent one final revision and was relaunched as the Mk III, which was to have total sales of 17,704. It boasted more power (up to 110.4kW/ 148bhp), was now built at Abingdon and was undoubtedly the best of the series, not to mention the fastest: its top speed was 194km/h (120mph).

However, when the company was faced with the need to modify the 3000 to meet US safety and emission controls in 1967, BMC decided that the costs were prohibitive and the axe fell; in 1968, just one car was assembled.

LOTUS ELITE

Country of origin: UK
Date: 1958
Engine: aluminium sohc inline
4-cylinder with SU carburettor,
producing 59.7kW (80bhp) at 6,100rpm
Transmission: 4-speed manual
Wheels driven: rear
Capacity: 1,216cc (74.2cu in)
Bore & stroke: 76.2 x 66.5mm (3 x 2.6in)
Performance: maximum speed
185km/h (115mph); 0–96.5km/h
(60mph) in 11.8 seconds
Dimensions: wheelbase 2.24m (7ft
4.2in); length 3.734m (12ft 3in);
width 1.4286m (4ft 10.5in); height
1.194m (3ft 11in); track 1.194m (3ft
11in) front, 1.224m (4ft 0.2in) rear
Kerb weight: 662.8kg (1,460lb)
Suspension: independent wishbones,
coil springs, tubular shock absorbers
and anti-sway bar front; independent
Chapman struts and trailing arm rear
Brakes: hydraulic; 4-wheel 241mm
(9.5in) discs
Compression ratio: 10 : 1

LOTUS SEVEN SERIES II

Country of origin: UK
Date: 1960
Engine: inline 4-cylinder with 8
overhead valves, producing 29.8kW
(40bhp) at 5,000rpm
Transmission: 4-speed manual
Wheels driven: rear
Capacity: 948cc (57.8cu in)
Bore & stroke: 63 x 76.2mm (2.5 x
3in)
Performance: maximum speed
136.8km/h (85mph); 0–96.5km/h
(60mph) in 14.3 seconds
Dimensions: wheelbase 2.235m (7ft
4in); length 3.353m (11ft); width
1.481m (4ft 10.3in); height 1.092m
(3ft 7in); track 1.232m (4ft 0.5in)
front and rear
Steering: rack and pinion
Kerb weight: 435.8kg (960lb)
Fuel: 22.7l (5gal/6US gal)
Suspension: coil springs front and
rear
Brakes: drums front and rear
Compression ratio: 8.3 : 1

Right: *a Caterham-produced Super
Seven, now a cult fun car*

This splendid two-seater coupé, with its unitary glass-fibre body, Coventry-Climax engine and Chapman struts at the rear has unarguably one of the industry's greatest shapes. Lotus has come a long way since Colin Chapman's first car of 1952, and along that way the Elite became his company's first serious road car.

It was designed by Chapman, John Frayling and Peter Kirwan-Taylor. Its fibreglass construction contributed greatly to the car's lightness, some of the 1,029 production run weighing in at a meagre 590kg (1,300lb). The superbly aerodynamic Elite featured a low-set oval air intake,

sloping bonnet, fixed plexiglass door windows and a very neatly cut off rear end. The first transmission was from the British Motor Corporation's MGA, though later models employed the German ZF unit. The suspension was borrowed from the Lotus Twelve racing car. Second-series cars adopted a revised rear suspension, with a simple wishbone system joined to the chassis by a ball and socket joint.

The Coventry-Climax engine was offered in a range of power, from 52.9–78.4kW (71–105bhp), but always sounded noisy in the spartan cockpit. The Elite was wondrous to look at, and even better to drive, with virtually no body roll.

The Colin Chapman Lotus Seven made its début in 1957. It was a revamped version of the Mk VI, Lotus' first production car of 1952–6 but had a new spaceframe and new suspension, hydraulic drum brakes and a choice of engines, though usually the 1,172cc (71.5cu in) Ford side-valve 100E engine was selected. With a 1,098cc

(66.9cu in) Coventry-Climax FWA engine fitted, the car was known as the Super Seven.

The Series I had an alloy nosecone and cycle wings; hence the reference to its being a 'motorcycle on four wheels'. There were no doors to this very basic model, but it did have a hood, complete with leaks.

The Series II was introduced in 1960, after 2+2 Series Is had been produced. It had a simplified spaceframe, with a revised suspension geometry. Cars for the home market had aluminium mudguards, but flowing fibreglass wings were used on those for North America and became standard for the Series II. The Ford 948cc (57.8cu in) engine became the standard power block from 1960, and from 1961 a 1,340cc (81.7cu in) Ford 109E engine was fitted.

Since 1973, Caterham has been the only authorised maker of the Lotus Seven.

MARCOS GT

Country of origin: UK
Date: 1960
Engine: Ford inline 4-cylinder with 8 overhead valves and a single carburettor, producing 29.1kW (39bhp) at 5,000rpm
Transmission: 4-speed manual
Wheels driven: rear
Capacity: 997cc (60.8cu in)
Bore & stroke: 80.9 x 48.4mm (3.19 x 1.91in)
Performance: maximum speed not known
Steering: rack and pinion
Suspension: double wishbones and coil springs front; coil springs, leading arms and Panhard rod at rear
Brakes: front discs, rear drums

Below: *the car driven by world champion Jackie Stewart*

The company was founded in 1959 by Jem **Mar**sh and Frank **Cos**tin, and its first car was of timber and plywood construction. Costin was soon to leave the company, and by 1968 the wooden monocoque had been abandoned, so as to enable Marcos to break into the big North American market. Ford Anglia 105E engines were used initially, but these were replaced by straight-six Volvo units, which were both heavy and expensive. Subsequently the company went into liquidation in 1971. The Marcos was reborn in 1981, when Jem Marsh Performance Cars was established.

The first Marcos was the gull-wing GT coupé with cycle mudguards, and was referred to by Frank Costin as a dry Lotus Seven; it entered production in 1960, and 29 had been produced by 1963 when it was replaced by the 1800.

The GT used the front suspension from the Triumph Herald, with all suspension components being bolted directly onto the wooden monocoque. There were fibreglass nosecones, which came in varying degrees of ugliness – part of the reason why the GT lacked popularity, although it did have a successful life on the circuits, especially in the hands of a young Jackie Stewart. Other engine options included the 405E bored out to 1,098cc (67cu in) or 1,148cc (70cu in) and Classic 1,340cc (81.8cu in) and 1,500cc (91.5cu in) blocks.

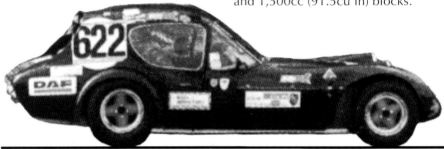

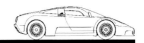

JAGUAR E-TYPE 3.8 ROADSTER

Country of origin: UK
Date: 1961
Engine: dohc inline 6-cylinder
Transmission: 4-speed manual
Wheels driven: rear
Capacity: 3,781cc (230.7cu in)
Bore & stroke: 87 x 106mm (3.4 x 4.2in)
Performance: maximum speed
244.1km/h (151.7mph); 0–96.5km/h
(60mph) in 6.9 seconds
Dimensions: wheelbase 2.438m (8ft);
length 4.453m (14ft 7.3in); width
1.656m (5ft 5.2in); height 1.219m
(4ft); track 1.27m (4ft 2in) front,
1.27m (4ft 2in) rear
Steering: rack and pinion
Kerb weight: 1,226.7kg (2,702lb)
Fuel: 63.7l (14gal/16.8US gal)
Suspension: independent torsion bars,
wishbones and anti-roll bar front;
independent double spring/shock units,
transverse lower links, longitudinal
radius arms and anti-roll bar rear
Brakes: all discs, rear inboard mounted
Compression ratio: 9 : 1

Three Le Mans victories made the exclusively racing model D-Type legendary, and led to the production of the 1957 XKSS model. However, only 16 of these were built owing to a fire which destroyed the production line. Once production restarted, the D-Type had evolved into the E-Type, the dream car of the early 1960s. At the time that it was announced the E was not only the most beautiful car in the world, but also it cost only about £2,000 ($5,600). It was sleek to the point of being a little cramped in the cockpit, but under the bonnet was the XK engine with triple SU carburettors, producing 197.6kW (265bhp) at 5,500rpm. It also had the traditional Jaguar large speedometer and rev counter mounted behind the stylish wood-trimmed wheel.

In addition to the 15,490 units sold of the 3.8-litre, which was available in both roadster and coupé forms, a limited lightweight variant was built between 1962 and 1964 for racing.

The 4.2 supplanted the 3.8 in 1965, with the ageing XK engine increased to 4,235cc (258.4cu in); 17,320 units were sold, and again both styles were available. A 2+2 coupé was added to the range in 1966, and sold 5,600 units. The 4.2 Series II was unveiled in 1969.

The exhilarating Series III, launched in 1971, was powered by the V12 5,343cc (326cu in) 202.8kW (272bhp) sohc engine and had many other refinements but disappeared from the production line in 1975.

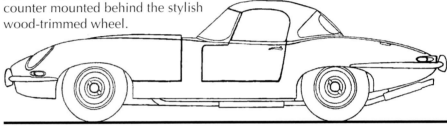

MG MIDGET

Country of origin: UK
Date: 1961
Engine: dohc inline 4-cylinder with cast-iron block with alloy head, producing 31kW (41.6bhp) at 5,500rpm
Transmission: 4-speed manual
Wheels driven: rear
Capacity: 948cc (57.8cu in)
Bore & stroke: 62.9 x 76.2mm (2.5 x 3in)
Performance: maximum speed 138.4km/h (86mph); 0–96.5km/h (60mph) in 20.2 seconds
Dimensions: wheelbase 2.032m (6ft 8in); length 3.467m (11ft 4.5in); width 1.346m (4ft 5in); height 1.262m (4ft 1.7in); track 1.161m (3ft 11.7in) front and 1.135m (3ft 8.7in) rear
Kerb weight: 705.5kg (1,554lb)
Fuel: 27.3l (6gal/7.2US gal)
Suspension: independent coil springs and wishbones front; live axle and semi-elliptic leaf springs rear; lever arm dampers front and rear
Brakes: Dunlop discs front and rear
Compression ratio: 9 : 1

Based on the successful Austin-Healey Sprite II, the Midget was promoted as the first MG model for 25 years to employ a power unit of under 1,000cc (61cu in).

The MG Midget Mk I was introduced in 1961, and sold over 25,000 units. It was replaced by the Mk II in 1964, which had a 1,098cc (67cu in) engine and sold only 2,500 units less, before making way for the Mk III in 1966. The Mk III was a disappointment, despite its 1,275cc (77.7cu in) engine which produced 48.3kW (65bhp), recording just under 13,500 sales before the Mk IV was introduced in 1969. The Mk IV really came into its own with new trim, black sills and Rostyle wheels. Over 86,500

units were sold of the Mk IV; the final Midget, the Mk V, which was produced between 1974 and 1979, reached sales of almost 74,000.

The Mk V had huge plastic bumpers and an increased ride height to meet US safety regulations. Unfortunately this adversely affected the handling. The Mk V also used the Triumph Spitfire 1,493cc (91cu in) engine and gearbox, which enabled it to be the first Midget to top 161km/h (100mph), and was undoubtedly the last true popular sports car of that era to have been mass-produced, retailing as new in 1975 at £1,559.61.

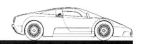

TRIUMPH TR4

Country of origin: UK
Date: 1961
Engine: inline 4-cylinder ohv with twin carburettors, producing 74.6kW (100bhp) at 4,600rpm
Transmission: 4-speed manual
Wheels driven: rear
Capacity: 2,138cc (130.4cu in)
Bore & stroke: 86 x 92mm (3.4 x 3.6in)
Performance: maximum speed 167.3km/h (104mph); 0–96.5km/h (60mph) in 10.9 seconds
Dimensions: wheelbase 2.235m (7ft 4in); length 3.835m (12ft 7in); width 1.461m (4ft 9.5in); height 1.27m (4ft 2in); track 1.27m (4ft 2in) front, 1.245m (4ft 1in) rear
Steering: rack and pinion
Kerb weight: 991kg (2,184lb)
Fuel: 53.5l (11.7gal/14.1US gal)
Suspension: coil springs front, leaf springs rear
Brakes: servo-assisted, discs front, drums rear
Compression ratio: 9 : 1

When the TR4 did eventually arrive, it proved to be no more than a rebodied version of what had been the highly successful 'interim' TR3A model. Styled by Michelotti, the TR4 gained an extra 305mm (12in) in overall length, on a 76mm (3in) wider track that definitely helped to improve the handling. It also afforded a roomier cockpit, though the ride remained uncompromisingly hard. Ironically, it was the TR4 that now became an interim model, ahead of the TR4A, which replaced

it on the production line in 1964. The latter remained in production until 1968. The TR4A looked little different externally, but under the bonnet the standard engine had been tweaked to produce a top speed of 177km/h (110mph); in addition and more importantly, there was a stiffer chassis with coil spring and semi-trailing link independent rear suspension.

However, the model began to lose sales because of its lack of power, and Standard Triumph had to look for a new power pack around which to launch a new model.

FERRARI 250 GTO

Country of origin: Italy
Date: 1962
Engine: sohc 60-degree V12 with 6 twin-choke Weber carburettors, producing 207kW (280bhp) at 7,500rpm
Transmission: 5-speed manual
Wheels driven: rear
Capacity: 2,953cc (180cu in)
Bore & stroke: 73 x 58.8mm (2.87 x 2.31in)
Performance: maximum speed 281.6km/h (175mph); 0–161km/h (100mph) in 14.1 seconds
Dimensions: wheelbase 2.6m (8ft 6.4in); length 4.399m (14ft 5.2in); width 1.674m (5ft 5.9in); height 1.245m (4ft 1in); track 1.351m (4ft 5.2in) front, 1.346m (4ft 5in) rear
Steering: recirculating ball
Kerb weight: 1,078kg (2,375lb)
Fuel: 143.8l (31.6gal/38US gal)
Suspension: independent double wishbone coil springs at front
Brakes: discs
Compression ratio: 9.8 : 1

Born out of a prototype run at Le Mans in 1961, the 250 GTO is perhaps the model which Ferrari enthusiasts hold most dear. It was that true Ferrari, a racing car that could be used on the road. Only 39 were built, yet the model became a legend in its own time and today commands the hightest of prices at auction.

It was the last Ferrari front-engined competition car, and is often referred to as Enzo's masterpiece. Its construction was based on the 250 GT SWB chassis of 1959–64, but with some lighter frame tubing to compensate for the increased size, and so gave a very rigid structure. A Porsche-patented all-synchro gearbox was coupled to the dry-sump Testarossa racing engine.

The initials stand for Gran Turismo Omologato, and the homologation rules normally call for 100 production-line vehicles to be manufactured. Enzo Ferrari was able to persuade the FIA to let him run the new-bodied SWBs, of which over 100 had already been manufactured, as a street car with an evolved body style.

The GTO was indeed strikingly different, with a low rounded nose and high clipped tail; it introduced a wedge-shape profile. Furthermore it was a winner on the track in its first year; it took first and second places at Silverstone and secured second place at Le Mans in the same year.

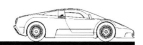

LOTUS ELAN

Country of origin: UK
Date: 1962
Engine: dohc inline 4-cylinder with a single carburettor, producing 78.3kW (105bhp) at 5,500rpm
Transmission: 4-speed manual
Wheels driven: rear
Capacity: 1,558cc (95.1cu in)
Bore & stroke: 82.6 x 72.6mm (3.2 x 2.9in)
Performance: maximum speed 172.2km/h (107mph); 0–96.5km/h (60mph) in 8.5 seconds
Dimensions: wheelbase 2.134m (7ft); length 3.688m (12ft 1.2in); width 1.422m (4ft 8in); height 1.143m (3ft 9in); track 1.194m (3ft 11in) front, 1.257m (4ft 1.5in) rear
Steering: rack and pinion
Kerb weight: 681kg (1,500lb)
Fuel: 45.4l (10gal/12US gal)
Suspension: coil springs front and rear
Brakes: discs front and rear
Compression ratio: 9.5 : 1

The Elite, introduced in 1957, had proved a financial disaster which almost bankrupted Lotus. It was complicated and costly to build, with only 998 units sold between its introduction and 1963.

In order to survive, Colin Chapman and his company turned their attention to a cheaper and more practical sports car, which would be powered by a new Lotus-built engine. The result was the Elan, and in contrast to the Elite, the Elan proved to be the making of the company.

The two-seater car was based on a simple pressed-steel backbone chassis, with a fibreglass shell. It

Right: *the Elan S4 Sprint, introduced in 1968, was considered to be the most desirable of the Elan series*

Below: *the 1990 version of Lotus' Elan SE, which was powered by a 16-valve 4-cylinder dohc Isuzu engine that produced 122kW (165bhp) when turbocharged*

emerged in 1962, initially as a roadster rag top, but a hard top soon followed. The car handled superbly, and its roadholding was outstanding; the Elan was a real classic in the making. It featured pop-up headlights, which were still something of a novelty in the UK, and its 'new' engine, which was the combination of a 4-cylinder British Ford block and a Lotus-designed twin-cam head, was to power all of the Elans. Nearly 8,000 were built between 1962 and 1969, including the S2, introduced in 1964, and the S3, introduced in 1966. The Elan+2 coupé replaced the S3; it was wider with a larger wheelbase, retained the original model's impeccable road manners and its build quality was considerably improved.

MGB ROADSTER

Country of origin: UK
Date: 1962
Engine: inline 4-cylinder ohv with twin SU HS4 carburettors, producing 70.8kW (95bhp) at 5,400rpm
Transmission: 4-speed manual
Wheels driven: rear
Capacity: 1,798cc (109.7cu in)
Bore & stroke: 80.3 x 89mm (3.2 x 3.5in)
Performance: maximum speed 168.9km/h (105mph); 0–96.5km/h (60mph) in 12.2 seconds
Dimensions: wheelbase 2.311m (7ft 7in); length 3.381m (12ft 9.2in); width 1.521m (4ft 11.9in); height 1.255m (4ft 1.4in); track 1.245m (4ft 1in) front and 1.25m (4ft 1.2in) rear
Steering: rack and pinion
Kerb weight: 940.7kg (2,072lb)
Fuel: 45.5l (10gal/12US gal)
Suspension: coil and wishbone front; live axle with leaf springs rear; lever arm dampers front and rear
Brakes: discs front, drums rear
Compression ratio: 8.8 : 1

The first MGB left the Abingdon factory in June 1962, and in one form or another the B remained in production until the latter's closure 18 years later.

The basic body of the MGB stayed the same throughout its production life, save for those large black plastic bumpers front and rear, that were added for 1975 models. It was MG's first car without a separate chassis and the monocoque construction allowed Abingdon to combine a reduction in overall length with an increase in passenger compartment size, when compared to the MGA.

No fewer than half a million MGBs were produced, of which 115,898 were the original MGB roadster units.

The MGB became an overnight success: affordable and practical, it was in effect a miniaturised estate car, with the rear seat back folding down to give a large luggage platform.

Other MGBs were the BGTs that were produced between 1965 and 1967; Mk II Bs and BGTs produced from 1967–74; the BGT V8 (1973–6) and the Mk II 'black-bumper' models produced from 1974–80.

The last MGB was completed at Abingdon on 22 October 1980, and thus ended over half a century of sports car motoring that had become synonymous with the MG marque.

TRIUMPH SPITFIRE

Country of origin: UK
Date: 1962
Engine: inline 4-cylinder ohv with twin carburettors, producing 47kW (63bhp) at 5,750rpm
Transmission: 4-speed manual
Wheels driven: rear
Capacity: 1,147cc (70cu in)
Bore & stroke: 69.3 x 76mm (2.7 x 3in)
Performance: maximum speed 151.2km/h (94mph); 0–96.5km/h (60mph) in 17.3 seconds
Dimensions: wheelbase 2.108m (6ft 11in); length 3.683m (12ft 1in); width 1.473m (4ft 10in); height 1.207m (3ft 11.5in); track 1.245m (4ft 1in) front, 1.219m (4ft) rear
Steering: rack and pinion
Kerb weight: 721.4kg (1,589lb)
Fuel: 37.5l (8.2gal/9.9US gal)
Suspension: coil springs front; leaf springs rear
Brakes: discs front, drums rear
Compression ratio: 9 : 1

Styled by Michelotti, who also styled the TR4, the Spitfire was Triumph's answer to the Sprite and was based around a rugged backbone chassis frame and a 4-cylinder 1.1-litre engine, which had been taken from the Triumph Herald 12/50 De Luxe. The steering was also Herald-based, as was the wheelbase, though for the Spitfire it was slightly shorter.

The body was a welded steel monocoque, and not only was the Spitfire a more elegant model than the competing Sprite, it was quicker, though like the TR4 its rear suspension still needed attention. The other advantages of the Spitfire were the larger cockpit and better equipmment and trim. The biggest advantage it enjoyed over its stablemate the TR4 was that it was nippy without feeling underpowered or heavy.

In 1965, the Spitfire was upgraded to Mk II with a few more horses and better quality trim. In 1967 the Mk III came along, with a new 1,296cc (79.1cu in) engine that produced 55.9kW (75bhp) and pushed the top speed to 161km/h (100mph) – just. It made way for the Mk IV in 1970, and when that passed away in 1974 it was replaced by the Spitfire 1500, *illustrated below*. Throughout its life, sales of the Spitfire had gone from strength to strength, with 45,000 for Mks I and II, 65,000 for Mk III, 70,000 for Mk IV and 95,000 for the 1500.

ASTON MARTIN DB5

Country of origin: UK
Date: 1963
Engine: dohc inline 6-cylinder with triple carburettors, producing 210.3kW (282bhp) at 5,500rpm
Transmission: 5-speed manual
Wheels driven: rear
Capacity: 3,995cc (243.7cu in)
Bore & stroke: 96 x 92mm (3.8 x 3.6in)
Performance: maximum speed 229.4km/h (142.6mph); 0–96.5km/h (60mph) in 8.1 seconds
Dimensions: wheelbase 2.489m (8ft 2in); length 4.610m (15ft 1.5in); width 1.676m (5ft 6in); height 1.334m (4ft 4.5in); track 1.372m (4ft 6in) front, 1.359m (4ft 5.5in) rear
Steering: rack and pinion
Kerb weight: 1,502kg (3,310lb)
Fuel: 100.1l (22gal/26.4US gal)
Suspension: coil springs front and rear
Brakes: power-assisted discs front and rear
Compression ratio: 8.9 : 1

Since the introduction of the DB4, continuing development had made necessary a new designation; thus the DB5, which was available from the autumn of 1963. It retained the basic chassis, body style and running gear of the later DB4 models, but apart from the very early production cars, all of the DB5s had all-synchromesh five-speed ZF gearboxes, and retained the DB4's faired-in headlights. A convertible version, known as the Volante, arrived in 1965. Since then, Aston Martin has retained this name for all of its rag tops.

A more powerful engine option became available under the new Vantage package from 1964, which employed a trio of twin-choke Weber carburettors to raise its power to 242.3kW (325bhp). Despite the DB5's starring role in the James Bond *Goldfinger* film, however, the car was fast falling behind the times. It had grown heavy – 181kg (400lb) more than the DB4 – and yet neither power steering nor air conditioning was available, and by the time that it was replaced by the DB6 in 1965, the future of the series was beginning to look uncertain, to say the least. Production of the model was 1,021 units, of which 123 were Volantes and a dozen were converted to shooting brakes by the coachbuilders Harold Radford.

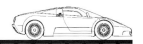

CHEVROLET CORVETTE STING RAY

Country of origin: USA
Date: 1963
Engine: sohc V8 with fuel-injection, producing 268.4kW (360bhp) at 6,000rpm
Transmission: 4-speed manual
Wheels driven: rear
Capacity: 5,363cc (327.2cu in)
Bore & stroke: 101.6 x 83.5mm (4 x 3.3in)
Performance: maximum speed 238.1km/h (148mph); 0–96.5km/h (60mph) in 6.5 seconds
Dimensions: wheelbase 2.489m (8ft 2in); length 4.45m (14ft 7.2in); width 1.765m (5ft 9.5in); height 1.245m (4ft 1in)
Steering: recirculating ball
Kerb weight: 1,474kg (3,248lb)
Fuel: 76l (16.7gal/20.1US gal)
Suspension: independent unequal-length A-arms, coil springs, tubular shock absorbers and anti-roll bar front; independent half-shafts, lateral arms, trailing radius rods, transverse semi-elliptic leaf springs and tubular shock absorbers rear
Brakes: hydraulic drums
Compression ratio: 11.2 : 1

Right: *an original 1963 Sting Ray*

Below: *a 1975 Stingray*

This all-new Corvette was a very different one, and probably the best. At its heart was the Corvette small-block V8, but enlarged from 4,638 to 5,363cc (283 to 327cu in). Its chassis was a new ladder frame, with a 101mm (4in) shorter wheelbase and independent rear suspension – a first for a modern US production car. Improved and enlarged drum brakes were still the norm, although discs were offered as an option from 1965. The stunning new body, though still fibreglass, was unlike that of any other production Corvette.

An amazing 117,964 units were produced between 1963 and 1967 when it was replaced by a revised model, which succeeded beyond

Chevrolet's wildest dreams. The Sting Ray name was dropped for production year 1968, when the model was known simply as the Corvette, and restored as a single word in 1969.

Cars from the model year 1963 are identifiable by a split rear window. Both coupé and roadster styles were available throughout the model's production life. Sting Rays sported smoother bonnets from 1965, and at the same time Chevrolet began to offer the first Corvette big-block V8. This was marketted as the Turbo-Jet, and was a 6,490cc (396cu in) wedge-head that produced 316.9kW (425bhp) at 6,400rpm; however, a 7-litre (427cu in) unit was offered for the following year.

FERRARI 500 SUPERFAST

Country of origin: Italy
Date: 1964
Engine: sohc V12, producing
268.4kW (360bhp) at 7,000rpm
Transmission: 4-speed manual with
overdrive
Wheels driven: rear
Capacity: 4,962cc (302.7cu in)
Bore & stroke: 87.9 x 68.1mm (3.5 x
2.7in)
Performance: maximum speed
265.5km/h (165mph); 0–96.5km/h
(60mph) in 6.6 seconds
Dimensions: wheelbase 2.598m (8ft
6.3in); length 4.77m (15ft 7.8in);
width 1.88m (6ft 2in); height 1.359m
(4ft 5.5in); track 1.483m (4ft 10.4in)
front, 1.478m (4ft 10.2in) rear
Kerb weight: 1,611kg (3,550lb)
Suspension: unequal-length A-arms
and coil springs front; live axle,
parallel trailing arms and semi-
elliptic leaf springs rear
Brakes: discs front and rear
Compression ratio: 8.8 : 1

*Below **and right:** **Series II models of
the 500 Superfast; the 5 in its
designation indicates its engine
capacity of almost 5 litres***

The 500 Superfast was Ferrari's
ultimate development of the America
line, and was unveiled at Geneva in
March 1964. The initial America
models had been followed first by the
410 Superamerica of 1956–9, then
came the 400 of 1960–4, by which
time the model had a long-wheelbase
chassis of 2.598m (8ft 6.3in). The
hood scoop had also been replaced
by a bulge over the carburettors.

Enter the Superfast in 1964, still a
two-seater, a little weightier and with
the wheelbase extended a little
farther. The Pininfarina body style
looked much like that of the 400
Superamerica, but it had open
headlights and lacked the squared-off
tail. Its refinement of comfort and

finish were such that it attracted the
label of Ferrari's Bugatti Royale.

By now the V12 engine had grown
to its largest incarnation but the bore
and stroke dimensions had reverted
to those of the 410. This was the
culmination of a long-running
succession; 25 units were built
initially, followed by a further 12
which became known as Series II
models and had five-speed manual
transmission. These also had new
engine mounts and suspended
pedals; externally they had different
side air vents and the 11 small
louvres of the initial batch were
replaced by larger vents. The model
was phased out in 1967.

The America line

The overall production numbers
were low, but there were thirteen
375 Americas produced between
1953 and 1955 sporting a wide
variety of bodies, including the
Pininfarina-fashioned cabriolet for
King Leopold of Belgium.

Ferrari introduced the 410
Superamerica in 1956, showing
the model at the Brussels motor
show in January with a 5-litre
engine tuned to 253.4kW

(340bhp) at 6,000rpm, initially using
the 375 chassis until switching to the
2.591m (8ft 6in) wheelbase chassis
from the 250 GT in 1957. The 410
lasted until 1959, being replaced by
the 400 Superamerica, 54 units of
which were made in total, including

all types. The 400 reverted to the
Colombo sohc V12, had overdrive
on the 4-speed box and was
capable of 257km/h (160mph).
Manufacture of all America and
Superamerica models reached
only 125 over 14 years, while
production of the 500 Superfast
ran at about one example per
month over its three-year span.

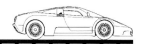

FORD MUSTANG

Country of origin: USA
Date: 1964
Engine: inline 6-cylinder ohv with a single carburettor, producing 89.5kW (120bhp) at 4,400rpm
Transmission: 3-speed automatic
Wheels driven: rear
Capacity: 3,277cc (199.9cu in)
Bore & stroke: 93.6 x 79.5mm (3.7 x 3.1 in)
Performance: maximum speed 144.8km/h (90mph); 0–96.5km/h (60mph) in 15.1 seconds
Dimensions: wheelbase 2.743m (9ft); length 4.613m (15ft 1.6in) width 1.732m (5ft 8.2in); height 1.298m (4ft 3.1in); track 1.407m (4ft 7.4in) front, 1.422m (4ft 8in) rear
Kerb weight: 1,212kg (2,670lb)
Fuel: 60.6l (13.3gal/16US gal)
Suspension: independent coil springs mounted over upper A-arms front; solid axle, longitudinal semi-elliptic leaf springs rear; tubular shock absorbers all round
Brakes: hydraulic; drums front and rear
Compression ratio: 9.2 : 1

The Thunderbird was launched in 1955, followed in 1958 by the four-seat Thunderbird. Both were heavy cars, constructed around the Ford high-performance V8 engine, and what Ford needed to counteract the flood of imported smaller sports models was a much cheaper model but with the long hood and short deck configuration of the T-bird.

Thanks to Lee Iacocca, this is exactly what arrived. The 6-cylinder hard-top 1965 model Mustang was introduced on 17 April 1964. Ford marketing and a huge range of optional extras that meant that your particular Mustang never looked the same as your neighbour's

did the rest. The planned annual sales projection of 100,000 units were sold within four months, and sales for the first 18 months topped 680,000.

Engine power was provided by the thin-wall Fairlane V8, the lightest cast-iron V8 on the market, which in its 271 Hi-Performance package pushed the top speed to 194km/h (120mph). Only minor or cosmetic alterations were made in the years that followed, apart from disc brakes, which were added nine months into production. The styles were originally hard top and rag top; a 2+2 (semi-fastback), with a folding rear seat, was added in the autumn of 1964.

PORSCHE 911

Country of origin: Germany
Date: 1964
Engine: sohc flat 6-cylinder, producing 108.1kW (145bhp) at 6,100rpm
Transmission: 5-speed manual
Wheels driven: rear
Capacity: 1,991cc (121.5cu in)
Bore & stroke: 80 x 66mm (3.1 x 2.6in)
Performance: maximum speed 212.4km/h (132mph); 0–96.5km/h (60mph) in 9 seconds
Dimensions: wheelbase 2.210m (7ft 3in); length 4.178m (13ft 8.5in); width 1.615m (5ft 3.6in); height 1.321m (4ft 4in); track 1.374m (4ft 8.1in) front, 1.316m (4ft 3.8in) rear
Steering: rack and pinion
Kerb weight: 1,071kg (2,360lb)
Fuel: 62.1l (13.6gal/16.4US gal)
Suspension: independent MacPherson struts, lower A-arms, longitudinal torsion bars front; independent semi-trailing arms, transverse torsion bars rear
Brakes: hydraulic; front and rear discs
Compression ratio: 9 : 1

A replacement for the 356, the 911 introduced a greater degree of comfort to a more practical design

Initially the 911 was broadly similar in layout and styling to the 356, with the gearbox ahead of the rear wheels and the engine behind them. More angular and 61mm (2.4in) narrower, it had full integral construction which provided more interior space.

A new Ferdinand Piech-designed flat-six air-cooled engine provided the power, and the transmission was borrowed from the 904 mid-engined sports racer that had been introduced the previous year.

The 911 became an instant success, and with constant updating and upgrading continues to be the cornerstone of Porsche production. It was renamed the 911L but this was not a different model. It gained a Weber carburettor from 1966.

The 911T Targa-top model came in 1967, powered by a two-litre (121cu in) engine, with the Sportomatic transmission becoming an option in 1968.

A hot version, the 911S, appeared in 1966 with a high-compression engine, fuel-injected from 1968. The touring car specification with a fuel-injected 115.6kW (155bhp) engine was introduced in 1968 as the 911E.

The first Porsche road car to have the 2.7-litre (165cu in) version of the flat-six engine and the tail aerofoil, the 911 Carrera, came in 1972. The Turbo version arrived in 1975, and in 1977 the version with the 3.3-litre (201cu in) engine.

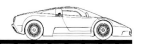

AC COBRA 427

Country of origin: UK/USA
Date: 1965
Engine: Ford V8 with a single carburettor, producing 290.8kW (390bhp) at 5,200rpm
Transmission: 4-speed manual
Wheels driven: rear
Capacity: 6,997cc (427cu in)
Bore & stroke: 101.6 x 72.9mm (4 x 2.9in)
Performance: maximum speed 265km/h (165mph); 0–96.5km/h (60mph) in 4.2 seconds
Dimensions: wheelbase 2.286m (7ft 6in); length 4.013m (13ft 2in); width 1.6m (5ft 3in); height 1.219m (4ft); track 1.359m (4ft 5.5in) front, 1.364m (4ft 5.7in) rear
Steering: rack and pinion
Kerb weight: 1,051kg (2,315lb)
Fuel: 68.2l (15gal/18US gal)
Suspension: coil springs front and rear
Brakes: hydraulic; discs front and rear
Compression ratio: 11 : 1

Founded in 1908, the AC company made a range of sports cars in small numbers, gaining a reputation for their quality. However, after the Second World War its models looked dated and its old-fashioned specifications failed to impress. The company began to slide into troubled waters.

The Ace model, launched in 1954, kept it going and brought it some limited success on the track on both sides of the Atlantic. However, even the Ace was beginning to show its age by the early 1960s. Just as things were becoming desperate Carroll Shelby came to the rescue, by fitting a 4-litre (244cu in) Ford engine into the Ace chassis to create the AC Cobra.

Shoe-horning the Ford Fairlane V8 into the Ace was no mean feat, and

AC was sending body and rolling chassis units to America by 1962. There in his Venice, California, garage Shelby weaved his magic.

Even so, although he sold only 654 units between 1962 and 1965, he created a Cobra with venom in 1965. In went the 6,996cc (427cu in) engine which produced 290.8kW (390bhp) at 5,200rpm to enable 0–161–0km/h (100mph) in a level 14 seconds; the 427 (*below*) was the ultimate Cobra. It was capable of 257km/h (160mph), but high insurance premiums and Government emission and safety controls combined to bury the model and by 1968 they had done just that.

Bottom: *a 289 MKII Cobra*

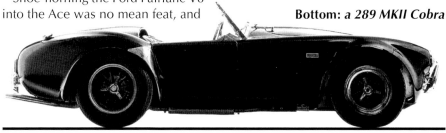

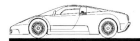

ASTON MARTIN DB6

Country of origin: UK
Date: 1965
Engine: dohc inline 6-cylinder with twin carburettors, producing 242.3kW (325bhp) at 5,750rpm
Transmission: 5-speed manual
Wheels driven: rear
Capacity: 3,995cc (243.7cu in)
Bore & stroke: 96 x 92mm (3.8 x 3.6in)
Performance: maximum speed 238.1km/h (148mph); 0–96.5km/h (60mph) in 6.5 seconds
Dimensions: wheelbase 2.565m (8ft 5in); length 4.623m (15ft 2in); width 1.676m (5ft 6in); height 1.372m (4ft 6in); track 1.372m (4ft 6in) front, 1.359m (4ft 5.5in) rear
Steering: rack and pinion
Kerb weight: 1,549kg (3,416lb)
Fuel: 100.1l (22gal/26.4US gal)
Suspension: coil springs front and rear
Brakes: discs front and rear
Compression ratio: 8.9 : 1

Aston Martin abandoned the DB5 after only two years, as a result of concern over its long-term viability. The plusher, but less sporty, DB6 was substituted yet failed to stop the rot. The company was selling primarily on its sporting ancestry, the previous decade having seen little by way of improved performance.

The DB6 retained the basic chassis design, now seven years old, but on a 95mm (3.75in) longer wheelbase and with a relocated rear axle. This stretch afforded additional back-seat space. The DB6 also made do with carryover running gear and suspension, along with the wire wheels, although at last power-assisted steering was listed as an option.

The windscreen was higher and more vertical, necessitating a raised roofline, but the aerodynamics were improved partly by the model's bobbed tail.

The Touring-patented *superleggera* method of construction was also forsaken; the new bodies were conventional with aluminium skins on steel inner panels, and there was a steel floor. When the DB6 ceased production in 1970, 1,567 units had been manufactured. With it ended a great line of cars which had begun with the DB2 of 1950, and it was to be another quarter of a century before the vastly different DB7 made its début.

SHELBY GT 350

Country of origin: USA
Date: 1965
Engine: V8 ohv with a single Holley carburettor, producing 228.2kW (306bhp) at 6,000rpm
Transmission: 4-speed manual
Wheels driven: rear
Capacity: 4,736cc (289cu in)
Bore & stroke: 101.6 x 72.9mm (4 x 2.9in)
Performance: maximum speed 199.5km/h (124mph); 0–96.5km/h (60mph) in 6.8 seconds
Dimensions: wheelbase 2.743m (9ft); length 4.613m (15ft 1.6in) width 1.732m (5ft 8.2in); height 1.3m (4ft 3.2in); track 1.435m (4ft 8.5in) front, 1.448m (4ft 9in) rear
Kerb weight: 1,266kg (2,790lb)
Suspension: independent upper wishbones, lower control arms and struts, coil springs and anti-roll bar front; rigid axle, semi-elliptic leaf springs and torque rods rear
Brakes: front discs, rear drums
Compression ratio: 11.2 : 1

Carroll Shelby was a successful racing driver who won at Le Mans in a Ferrari in 1959. Competition success in North America followed with the Cobra roadster, a car that was a marriage between the lightweight British AC Ace body and the Ford V8 small block (see page 75).

Shelby was asked by Ford to prepare a reasonably-priced high-speed version of the company's Mustang soon after its introduction. The company anticipated that if such a development should be successful, it would provide surefire high-profile publicity. It did not take Shelby long – in fact nothing ever did.

Ford shipped partially completed Mustang fastbacks, only in white, and without rear seats,

bonnets, and exhaust systems. Shelby tweaked Ford's engine, added a 4-barrel carburettor, a straight-through exhaust system and a fibreglass bonnet with a functional scoop.

Twelve basically 2+2 racers had been put together by Christmas 1964. Just a week later, the Shelby team had 100 Shelby Mustangs ready for the Sports Car Club of America to inspect for homologation purposes under production car racer rules.

The new car dominated its class from the beginning, winning a series of national championships which continued into the coming years. Sales, however, were never dramatic, reaching only a modest 562 units in 1965, and 2,378 the following year.

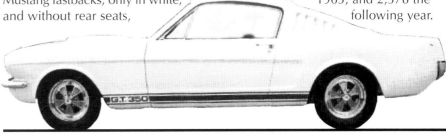

Above: *the original GT 350*   Below: *the larger and later GT 500*

FERRARI 275 GTB/4

Country of origin: Italy
Date: 1966
Engine: dohc 60-degree V12 with 6
Weber carburettors, producing
222kW (300bhp) at 8,000rpm
Transmission: 5-speed manual
Wheels driven: rear
Capacity: 3,286cc (200.5cu in)
Bore & stroke: 77 x 58.8mm (3.03 x
2.31in)
Performance: maximum speed
249.4km/h (155mph); 0–161km/h
(100mph) in 15 seconds
Dimensions: wheelbase 2.4m (7ft
10.5in); length 4.409m (14ft 5.6in);
width 1.725m (5ft 7.9in); height
1.245m (4ft 1in); track 1.401m (4ft
7.2in) front, 1.417m (4ft 7.8in) rear
Steering: worm and roller
Kerb weight: 1,114kg (2,455lb)
Fuel: 93.9l (20.6gal/24.8US gal)
Suspension: independent double
wishbones and coil springs front and rear
Brakes: discs front and rear
Compression ratio: 9.2 : 1

Both the GTB and the GTS model
275s, developments of the 250GT,
appeared in 1964. They both had
short wheelbases, all-independent
suspension – a far superior system
technically to any previous roadgoing
Ferrari – and five-speed transaxles.

The GTB (Berlinetta) fastback coupé
was intended as a road car/racer, with
the engine producing 208.8kW
(280bhp), while the GTS (Spyder)
convertible was a road car. The GTB
had enclosed headlights, the GTS
(*illustrated*) open ones, and the
GTB had a lower bank of four
rectangular air intakes

along its sleekly aerodynamic shape
which were quite different to those
on the GTS. The seriously sporting
preferred the lightweight GTB/C, and
when twin-overhead camshafts
appeared for the first time on a
production Ferrari in 1966, the cars
were designated GTB/4.

Production of the GTS ran to 200
units; of the GTB about 450 between
1964 and 1966 and of the GTB/4 about
280 units between 1966 and 1968.

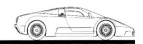

FORD GT40

Country of origin: UK
Date: 1966
Engine: mid-mounted V8 ohv, producing 249.8kW (335bhp) at 6,250rpm
Transmission: 5-speed manual
Wheels driven: rear
Capacity: 4,736cc (289cu in)
Bore & stroke: 101.7 x 72.9mm (4 x 2.9in)
Performance: maximum speed 263.9km/h (164mph); 0–96.5km/h (60mph) in 5.3 seconds
Dimensions: wheelbase 2.413m (7ft 11in); length 4.181m (13ft 8.6in) width 1.778m (5ft 10in); height 1.029m (3ft 4.5in); track 1.372m (4ft 6in) front and rear
Steering: rack and pinion
Kerb weight: 930kg (2,050lb)
Fuel: 140l (30.8gal/37US gal)
Suspension: all-independent coil springs front and rear
Brakes: discs front and rear
Compression ratio: 9.1 : 1

Ford UK was founded in Manchester in 1911, to assemble US-produced Model T components. The company rapidly became the largest European car maker before opening its factory at Dagenham for the production of the Model Y. It produced engines, especially the 997cc (60.8cu in) 105E, which were extensively used by smaller builders and tuners, and became the basis of Lotus Formula Junior success.

Ford entered motorsport in the 1960s, in an attempt to improve its salesroom image. It launched the GT40 in 1966, aiming it specifically at winning the Le Mans 24-Hour race, and its name was derived from its height of 1.016m (40 inches). Ford Advanced Vehicles built 107 GT40s in total at Slough, of which 31 were delivered for road use. A works-entered car managed a top speed of more than 322km/h (200mph) at Le Mans, and a Mk 2 won there in 1966.

The Mk 3 was intended to be the definitive road car, with a detuned 228.2kW (306bhp) engine. It was better equipped and roomier, with a central gear shift. However, policy changes prevented the initial run of 20 planned units extending to more than seven before the model was shelved.

JENSEN INTERCEPTOR

Country of origin: UK
Date: 1966
Engine: V8 ohv with a single
carburettor, producing 242.3kW
(325bhp) at 4,600rpm
Transmission: Chrysler Torqueflite
3-speed automatic
Wheels driven: rear
Capacity: 6,276cc (382.9cu in)
Bore & stroke: 108 x 86mm (4.2 x 3.4in)
Performance: maximum speed
214km/h (133mph); 0–96.5km/h
(60mph) in 7.3 seconds
Dimensions: wheelbase 2.667m (8ft
9in); length 4.775m (15ft 8in); width
1.753m (5ft 9in); height 1.346m (4ft
5in); track 1.422m (4ft 8in) front,
1.448m (4ft 9in) rear
Steering: power-assisted rack and pinion
Kerb weight: 1,678kg (3,697lb)
Fuel: 72.8l (16gal/19.2US gal)
Suspension: coil springs front; leaf
springs rear
Brakes: discs front and rear
Compression ratio: 10 : 1

Jensen first pioneered all-wheel drive road cars with ABS anti-lock braking systems years ahead of the rest of the world with the FF in 1966, the same year as the launch of the rear-wheel drive Interceptor, its second model of that name. Externally, the Interceptor was identifiable only by the single cooling vent in the side panels; the FF had two. Both models shared the 6,276cc (382.9cu in) V8 ohv engine, and although the FF was available as a two-door sports saloon only, the Interceptor was also available as a two-door coupé or convertible. The FF stood for Ferguson Formula. Vignale styled the hatchback body for the model, and Chrysler supplied the engine.

The Mk I Interceptor made way for the Mk II in 1970. This had a revised dash and a slightly altered front; the Mk III took over in 1972. This had vented disc brakes and alloy wheels.

The gas-guzzling Interceptor was available between 1966 and 1976, during which time 6,175 units were sold. A bigger 7.2-litre (444.6cu in) engine was available from 1971. This had triple twin-choke carburettors, produced 278kW (385bhp) and was marketted as the SP.

The convertible was available from 1974, and the coupé from 1975. The model saw off two oil crises and a world recession but Jensen filed for bankruptcy in 1975 and closed its doors in May, 1976.

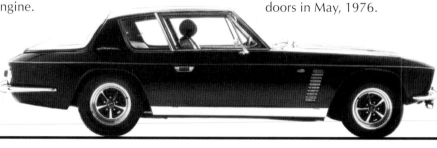

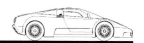

LOTUS EUROPA

Country of origin: UK
Date: 1966
Engine: rear-mounted inline 4-cylinder ohv with a single carburettor, producing 61.1kW (82bhp) at 6,500rpm
Transmission: 4-speed manual
Wheels driven: rear
Capacity: 1,470cc (89.7cu in)
Bore & stroke: 76 x 81mm (3 x 3.2in)
Performance: maximum speed 175.4km/h (109mph); 0–96.5km/h (60mph) in 11.2 seconds
Dimensions: wheelbase 2.311m (7ft 7in); length 3.993m (13ft 1.2in); width 1.638m (5ft 4.5in); height 1.08m (3ft 6.5in); track 1.346m (4ft 5in) front and rear
Steering: rack and pinion
Kerb weight: 662kg (1,460lb)
Fuel: 34.1l (7.5gal/9US gal)
Suspension: independent coil springs front and rear
Brakes: front discs, rear drums
Compression ratio: 10.3 : 1

The advent of the front-wheel drive Renault 16 enabled Lotus to produce its first mid-engined GT. It did this by purchasing the transaxle and the 58.1kW (78bhp) engine, turning the axle through 180 degrees, and re-mating it to a modified transaxle, in return for Renault's co-operation. Sales for the first two years were to be limited to Europe; thus was born the Europa.

Its powertrain sat north-south behind the cockpit, but ahead of the back wheels and like other roadgoing Lotuses, it had a fibreglass body atop a steel backbone frame. The chassis was similar to that of the Elan and had the body bonded onto it.

The Europa's performance was not outstanding and the cockpit was rather cramped; as with previous Lotus models, it all too frequently suffered from inferior build quality. The S2 was introduced in 1968, with the body now bolted on, and the US market received the larger 1,545cc (94.3cu in) Renault 16TS engine. The S3 Twin-Cam, with a 78.3kW (105bhp) Lotus-Ford dohc 4-cylinder appeared in 1971. This model also benefitted from improved rear vision and had a top speed of 194km/h (120mph).

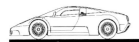

ALFA ROMEO 1750 SPYDER VELOCE

Country of origin: Italy
Date: 1967
Engine: dohc inline 4-cylinder with fuel injection, producing 98.4kW (132bhp) at 5,500rpm
Transmission: 5-speed manual
Wheels driven: rear
Capacity: 1,779cc (108.5cu in)
Bore & stroke: 80 x 88.5mm (3.1 x 3.5in)
Performance: maximum speed 185km/h (115mph); 0–96.5km/h (60mph) in 9.9 seconds
Dimensions: wheelbase 2.25m (7ft 4.6in); length 4.265m (13ft 11.9in); width 1.631m (5ft 4.2in); height 1.29m (4ft 2.8in); track 1.311m (4ft 3.6in) front, 1.27m (4ft 2in) rear
Steering: worm and sector
Kerb weight: 1,065kg (2,346lb)
Fuel: 46.2l (10.1gal/12.2US gal)
Suspension: coil springs front and rear
Brakes: discs front and rear
Compression ratio: 9.5 : 1

Despite Alfa's dominance of the endurance events during the inter-war years, the company was mainly an aero-engine manufacturer, only turning to volume car production in the 1950s. It launched the Duetto, which also became known as the Guilia Sprint Spyder, in 1966. This was styled by Pininfarina, and its simple body lines with the low grille and the inbuilt bumpers heralded a modern classic, a version of which was to remain in production for decades to come. Its power came from the 81.25kW (109bhp) Guilia engine, but after a production run of 6,325 the model was replaced in 1967 by the 1750 Spyder Veloce.

This new model also had the same chopped-off tail style, and retained the earlier construction and suspension layout. It came at a time when reasonably-priced mass-produced open sports cars were becoming a rarity.

Production of the two-seater convertible 1750 continued until 1971, when it made way for what has become the ultimate incarnation of the Duetto, the 2000 Spyder Veloce. This developed rubber bumpers during the 1980s, but in 1990 had a makeover that included revised tail treatment and discreet new bumpers, colour-keyed to the bodywork.

The first production of the 2000 had a 1,962cc (120cu in) version of the 1962 Guilia 4-cylinder engine, and during the 1990s it retained the inline four but with fuel injection and two valves per cylinder, producing 89.5kW (120bhp) at 5,800rpm. The transmission remained five-speed manual, and the top speed little changed at 191.5km/h (119mph).

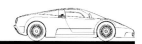

LAMBORGHINI MIURA

Country of origin: Italy
Date: 1967
Engine: transversely mid-mounted dohc V12 with 6 carburettors, producing 242.3kW (325bhp) at 7,000rpm
Transmission: 5-speed manual
Wheels driven: rear
Capacity: 3,929cc (239.7cu in)
Bore & stroke: 82 x 62mm (3.2 x 2.4in)
Performance: maximum speed 289.6km/h (180mph); 0–96.5km/h (60mph) in 5.5 seconds
Dimensions: wheelbase 2.466m (8ft 1.1in); length 4.348m (14ft 3.2in); width 1.763m (5ft 9.4in); height 1.09m (3ft 6.9in); track 1.4m (4ft 7.1in) front, 1.514m (4ft 11.6in) rear
Steering: rack and pinion
Kerb weight: 1,289kg (2,840lb)
Fuel: 79.5l (17.5gal/21.6US gal)
Suspension: upper and lower A-arms, coil springs, tubular shock absorbers and anti-roll bars front and rear
Brakes: hydraulic; discs front and rear
Compression ratio: 10.7 : 1

Ever since it began building cars, Lamborghini has maintained a reputation for style; producing *the* Italian dream cars. Unfortunately mechanical competence was never its forte, and consequently it has not made its owners rich.

Lamborghini launched its 350GT in 1964 as a competitor to those other Italian high-rollers of the early 1960s, the Ferrari 400 and Maserati Sebring. It was powered by a 208.7kW (280bhp)

3.5-litre (213.5cu in) dohc V12 engine. This model was followed by the 400GT, which together with the Miura put Lamborghini on the map.

The Miura made its fully-bodied but otherwise unfinished début at the Geneva show in 1966. This shell was breathtaking, and astonished the motoring world; it was straight out of tomorrow. The shape is credited to Bertone's Marcello Gandini.

The engine exhibited amazing flexibility, and if the car did have a major fault it was its tendency to lift at high speed but its myriad minor irritations were suffered gladly by the 765 Miura owners.

FERRARI 365 GTB/4 'Daytona'

Country of origin: Italy
Date: 1968
Engine: dohc 60-degree V12 with 6 Weber 40 DCN 20 carburettors, producing 262.6kW (352bhp) at 7,500rpm
Transmission: 5-speed manual
Wheels driven: rear
Capacity: 4,390cc (267.9cu in)
Bore & stroke: 81 x 71mm (3.2 x 2.8in)
Performance: maximum speed 278.4km/h (173mph); 0–96.5km/h (60mph) in 5.9 seconds
Dimensions: wheelbase 2.4m (7ft 10.5in); length 4.425m (14ft 6.2in); width 1.76m (5ft 9.3in); height 1.245m (4ft 1in); track 1.44m (4ft 8.7in) front, 1.425m (4ft 8.1in) rear
Steering: recirculating ball
Kerb weight: 1,634kg (3,600lb)
Fuel: 99.9l (22gal/26.4US gal)
Suspension: independent double wishbones and coil springs front and rear
Brakes: discs front and rear
Compression ratio: 8.8 : 1

The Daytona, so-called by the press rather than Maranello, is one of the all-time great Ferraris. It is also one of the company's most remarkable roadgoing models. When first shown at the Paris motor show in 1968, it was not only the costliest Ferrari to date, but also the fastest.

Built on the 275 chassis, including its wheelbase and rear-transaxle configuration, the body was married to an evolutionary version of the Columbo V12 engine that was bored to 4.4-litre capacity. This superb dry-sumped quad-cam engine with 6 twin-choke Weber carburettors produced 262.6kW (352bhp).

Styled by Pininfarina, the Daytona

has become legendary, with its exaggerated long-hood and short-deck proportions. It was Ferrari's answer to the Lamborghini Miura, and just as the Miura encountered problems, so did the Daytona, which was difficult in the extreme to drive fast; it was overweight and the disc brakes were just not up to the job.

It was strictly a two-seater, and was available in either coupé or spyder style (GTS/4). The sales of each were about 1,280 and 125 respectively, over its four-year production cycle. Sadly, as magnificent as it was, the car proved to be Maranello's last expression of the traditional *gran turismo*.

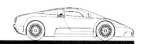

MORGAN PLUS EIGHT

Country of origin: UK
Date: 1968
Engine: Rover V8 ohv with twin carburettors, producing 119.7kW (160.5bhp) at 5,200rpm
Transmission: 4-speed manual
Wheels driven: rear
Capacity: 3,529cc (215.3cu in)
Bore & stroke: 88.9 x 71.1mm (3.5 x 2.8in)
Performance: maximum speed 201.1km/h (125mph); 0–96.5km/h (60mph) in 6.7 seconds
Dimensions: wheelbase 2.489m (8ft 2in); length 3.861m (12ft 8in); width 1.448m (4ft 9in); height 1.27m (4ft 2in); track 1.245m (4ft 1in) front, 1.295m (4ft 3in) rear
Steering: worm and nut
Kerb weight: 898kg (1,979lb)
Fuel: 61.4l (13.5gal/16.2US gal)
Suspension: coil springs front; leaf springs rear
Brakes: front discs, rear drums
Compression ratio: 10.5 : 1

Morgan continued the theme of its 4/4 and Plus Four models with Series II and III 4/4 models in 1955 and 1960, and in the latter year also a Plus Four Supersport. Series IV and V 4/4 models followed in 1962 and 1963 respectively, and the Plus Four Plus again in 1963. The 4/4 1600 was well received when it was launched in 1967 with its new 1,599cc (97.5cu in) Ford Kent engine.

The Plus Four name was revived in 1988 when the 4/4 was offered with the option of the 2-litre (122cu in) dohc Rover M16 engine. Another Rover engine, the 3.5-litre (215.3cu in) V8, was put at the heart of the Plus Eight, which was introduced in 1968 when the ageing TR engine,

used on the 1954 Plus Four, needed replacement.

The Rover M16 had an aluminium block of compact dimensions, which presented Morgan with no fitting problems, although 51mm (2 inches) was added to the wheelbase. Since its introduction in 1968, the Plus Eight has benefitted from increased power, currently a 3,946cc (240.7cu in) V8 producing 140kW (190bhp) at 4,750rpm. The Plus Eight may be distinguished by its cast-alloy wheels, a more ground-hugging stance and by wider bumpers.

This model still retains the traditional Morgan characteristics of poor aerodynamics, rudimentary weather protection, jolting ride and minimal space, which all add to its charm.

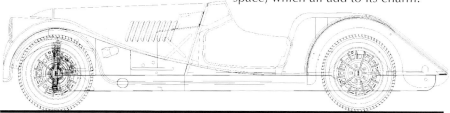

FERRARI DINO 246 GT

Country of origin: Italy
Date: 1969
Engine: transversely mid-mounted
dohc V6 with 3 carburettors, pro-
ducing 130.5kW (175bhp) at 7,000rpm
Transmission: 5-speed manual
Wheels driven: rear
Capacity: 2,418cc (147.5cu in)
Bore & stroke: 92.5 x 60mm (3.64 x 2.4in)
Performance: maximum speed
226.9km/h (141mph); 0–96.5km/h
(60mph) in 7.9 seconds
Dimensions: wheelbase 2.339m (7ft
8.1in); length 4.201m (13ft 9.4in);
width 1.702m (5ft 7in); height
1.133m (3ft 8.6in); track 1.427m (4ft
8.2in) front, 1.43m (4ft 8.3in) rear
Steering: rack and pinion
Kerb weight: 1,257kg (2,770lb)
Fuel: 70.4l (15.5gal/18.6US gal)
Suspension: unequal-length A-arms,
coil springs, tubular shock absorbers
and anti-roll bars front and rear
Brakes: hydraulic discs front and rear
Compression ratio: 9 : 1

The first Dino Ferrari was the 206, which was launched in 1967. It took its name from the small capacity V6 engine that had been named for Enzo's son, who before his death in 1956 had had some input into the design, under the supervision of the great Italian designer Vittorio Jano.

The engine had already been proved in F1 and F2 sports car racing, and was rated at 134.2kW (180bhp). It was mounted transversely amidships in this first baby Ferrari. The styling of the 206 was by Pininfarina, but it did not carry a Ferrari badge. The Dino was launched as a separate marque, with Fiat building a large part of the engine; Fiat took a controlling interest in Ferrari from 1969.

This first roadgoing Dino never sold well, being uncomfortable and noisy. The 246 GT did much better, with approximately 2,800 units being sold between 1969 and 1973. It still provided a noisy ride, even though the 2.4-litre (147.5cu in) engine was much quieter.

The GTS (S for Spyder, although this version was actually a Targa-top) arrived in 1972 but, like the 206, the 246 Dino models never received their Ferrari insignia although today you might well find that they have been added by their owners. The 246 was replaced by the larger 208 and 308 Dino GT4 models in 1973, with their new 2 or 3-litre V8 engines and 2+2 seating.

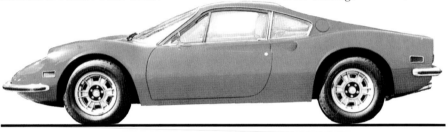

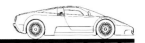

DATSUN 240Z

Country of origin: Japan
Date: 1970
Engine: inline 6-cylinder with twin carburettors, producing 111.9kW (150bhp) at 6,000rpm
Transmission: 4-speed manual
Wheels driven: rear
Capacity: 2,393cc (146cu in)
Bore & stroke: 83 x 73.3mm (3.3 x 2.9in)
Performance: maximum speed 196.3km/h (122mph); 0–96.5km/h (60mph) in 8.7 seconds
Dimensions: wheelbase 2.304m (7ft 6.7in); length 4.135m (13ft 6.8in); width 1.628m (5ft 4.1in); height 1.285m (4ft 2.6in); track 1.354m (4ft 5.3in) front, 1.346m (4ft 5in) rear
Kerb weight: 1,069kg (2,355lb)
Fuel: 60.2l (13.2gal/15.9US gal)
Suspension: MacPherson struts, lower wishbones, coil springs and anti-roll bar front; Chapman struts, lower wishbones, coil springs and anti-roll bar rear
Brakes: front discs, rear drums
Compression ratio: 9 : 1

Nissan's first serious attempt to create a sports car was the Fairlady, which was launched in 1961, initially with a 1,488cc (90.8cu in) engine. An upgrade to 1,596cc (97.4cu in) became available from 1964, but the top of the Fairlady range was the Datsun 2000, launched in 1967 and powered by an sohc 1,982cc (120.9cu in) 4-cylinder engine.

The Fairlady line was replaced in 1969 by the Fairlady Z series. This became better known as the Datsun 240Z and was to establish Nissan in North America. The 240Z burst onto the American scene, taking the market by surprise and the Americans reacted to it with enthusiasm. It soon began to outsell the British imports

such as the Austin-Healey 3000, MGB and Jaguar E-Type on price, the specification (which included optional automatic transmission) and the level of trim.

Nissan coped with the US safety and emission requirements by introducing the 260Z. It appeared with a 2,565cc (156.5cu in) engine in 1973, and the 2+2 280Z was introduced in 1975 with power provided by a 2,753cc (168cu in) engine. The total production of the range reached 622,649 units before being replaced in 1978 by the fuel-injected 280ZX. The 240Z had contributed 156,078 examples to this quantity, making it the world's best-selling sports model.

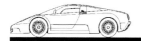

DE TOMASO PANTERA

Country of origin: Italy
Date: 1971
Engine: Ford V8 ohv with a single carburettor, producing 231.2kW (310bhp) at 5,400rpm
Transmission: ZF 5-speed manual
Wheels driven: rear
Capacity: 5,763cc (351.6cu in)
Bore & stroke: 102 x 89mm (4 x 3.5in)
Performance: maximum speed 207.6km/h (129mph); 0–96.5km/h (60mph) in 6.8 seconds
Dimensions: wheelbase 2.499m (8ft 2.4in); length 4.252m (13ft 11.4in); width 1.811m (5ft 11.3in); height 1.12m (3ft 8.1in); track 1.448m (4ft 9in) front, 1.461m (4ft 9.5in) rear
Steering: rack and pinion
Kerb weight: 1,432kg (3,155lb)
Fuel: 79.5l (17.5gal/21US gal)
Suspension: upper and lower wishbones, coil springs, tubular shock absorbers and anti-roll bar front and rear
Brakes: hydraulic; discs front and rear
Compression ratio: 11 : 1

Argentinian racing driver Alejandro de Tomaso established his company in the heartland of Italian sports car production at Módena. Not content with his own brand, he also acquired the prestigious marques of Maserati and Innocenti, along with the styling houses of Vignale and Ghia, and then just for good measure he added the motorcycle makers Benelli and Moto Guzzi.

The first De Tomaso road car model was the Vallelunga, which made its début in 1965. It was followed by the Mangusta in 1967, which utilised the Vallelunga chassis and Ford's 4.7-litre V8, which delivered 228.2kW (306bhp) and claimed a top speed of 250km/h (155mph).

The Pantera, which replaced the Mangusta in 1971, was the first affordable mid-engined exotic. It was produced to a far higher quality build than previous de Tomaso models, thanks to imput from Ford's Lee Iacocca, and the car was designed specifically for the North American market.

The pressed-steel unitary chassis was designed by Giampaolo Dallara. The engine, originally from the USA, was made by Ford Australia from 1980.

Over the years de Tomaso has shed his other automobile interests and his only production car today remains the Pantera, which continues to sell in limited numbers.

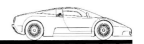

FIAT X1/9

Country of origin: Italy
Date: 1972
Engine: sohc inline 4-cylinder with 8 valves and a single Weber carburettor, mounted transversely behind the driver, producing 54.4kW (73.0bhp) at 6,000rpm
Transmission: 4-speed manual
Wheels driven: rear
Capacity: 1,290cc (78.7cu in)
Bore & stroke: 86 x 55.5mm (3.4 x 2.2in)
Performance: maximum speed 160.9km/h (100mph); 0–96.5km/h (60mph) 12.7 seconds
Dimensions: wheelbase 2.202m (7ft 2.7in); length 3.82m (12ft 6.7in); width 1.567m (5ft 1.7in); height 1.168m (3ft 10in); track 1.334m (4ft 4.5in)
Steering: rack and pinion
Kerb weight: 913kg (2,011lb)
Fuel: 47.8 litres (10.5gal/12.6 US gal)
Suspension: independent MacPherson struts and lower wishbones front; independent MacPherson struts, wishbones and single links rear
Brakes: discs front and rear
Compression ratio: 8.5 : 1

Below: a Bertone-badged X1-9 which was powered by the Ritmo 1,498cc (91.4cu in) engine that had been mounted transversely behind the driver

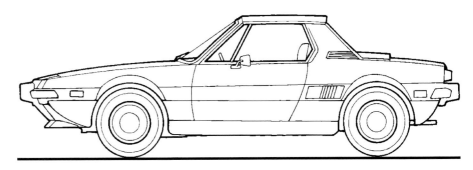

Fiat was established a century ago in 1899. It was a vast combine with a variety of interests and its early cars were aimed squarely at the middle market; after the First World War they became Italy's most popular make. Over the years the company has acquired a number of other marques and in the process has become a truly multinational corporation.

Fiat's efforts after the Second World War included the limited-production V8 and 1100 Transformabile sports car models, followed by the mass-produced, Pininfarina-designed 1200 range. The latter appeared in 1959, and were followed by the 850 Spyder styled by Bertone, the 124 Spyder and the 124 Abarth Rallye.

The Dino Coupé, which was powered by Ferrari's front mounted 1,987cc (121cu in) dohc Dino V6 engine delivering 118kW (160bhp), preceded Fiat's last entry into the sports car market in 1972. The X1/9 was the most successful mass-produced mid-engined sports car, with sales in excess of 180,000 units.

The Targa-topped body had been designed by Marcello Gandini at Bertone, best known for the lines of the sensational Miura, and the car was launched with the 1,290cc (78.7cu in) 4-cylinder engine from the Fiat 128 saloon, together with the 128 gearbox. Its handling and road-holding were both excellent, but the car cried out for more power. This became available in 1980, when the 1,499cc (91.5cu in) power pack and five-speed gearbox from the Ritmo and Strada models were utilised. This engine provided 63.3kW (85bhp) in the European and 49.9kW (67bhp) for the American version. Its highest speed was 170km/h (106mph), and 0–96.5km/h (60mph) time was 11 seconds. The model continued in production until 1982, when it was taken over by Bertone as the X1-9, and manufac-tured until 1989.

The Fiat X1/9 was the only low-priced sports car of the 1970s, and showed how a transverse rear wheel drive arrangement could be used to create a practical mid-engined sports car in the same class as the Sprite, Midget and Spitfire.

LANCIA STRATOS

Country of origin: Italy
Date: 1973
Engine: mid-mounted Ferrari Dino quad overhead cam 65-degree V6 with triple Weber carburettors, producing 141.7kW (190bhp) at 7,000rpm
Transmission: 5-speed manual
Wheels driven: front
Capacity: 2,418cc (147.5cu in)
Bore & stroke: 92.5 x 60mm (3.64 x 2.36in)
Performance: maximum speed 230km/h (143mph); 0–96.5km/h (60mph) in 6.8 seconds
Dimensions: wheelbase 2.172m (7ft 1.5in);length 3,711m (12ft 2.1in); track 1.432m (4ft 8.4in) front, 1.46m (4ft 9.5in) rear
Steering: rack and pinion
Kerb weight: 980kg (2,160lb)
Suspension: upper and lower A-arms, coil springs and anti-roll bar front and rear; Chapman struts rear
Brakes: discs front and rear

The Stratos was developed as a homologation special for European rallying. It was initially unreliable, but grew to become a cult car and won the World Rally Championship in both 1975 and 1976. Today it is regarded as a modern classic.

It was a two-seater coupé built around a simple steel monocoque with a fibreglass body, independent suspension and 4-wheel disc brakes.

Fiat took over Lancia in 1969, and also acquired a half-share in Ferrari.

It should be no surprise, therefore, that the midships drivetrain of the Stratos was

lifted intact from Ferrari's Dino 246 GT.

Having displayed a protype at the Turin motor show in November 1971, Lancia built 500 units of the planned production run between 1973 and 1975. Created by Bertone, the car was chunky and stubby and featured semi-concealed A-pillars and bold upswept contours, incorporating huge front wheel arches.

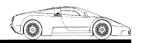

LAMBORGHINI COUNTACH LP400

Country of origin: Italy
Date: 1974
Engine: mid-mounted dohc V12 with 6 carburettors, producing 279.6kW (375bhp) at 8,000rpm
Transmission: 5-speed manual
Wheels driven: rear
Capacity: 3,929cc (239.7cu in)
Bore & stroke: 82 x 62mm (3.2 x 2.4in)
Performance: maximum speed 308.9km/h (192mph); 0–96.5km/h (60mph) in 6.8 seconds
Dimensions: wheelbase 2.451m (8ft 0.5in); length 4.14m (13ft 7in); width 1.89m (6ft 4.4in); height 1.069m (3ft 6.1in); track 1.501m (4ft 11.1in) front, 1.519m (4ft 11.8in) rear
Steering: rack and pinion
Kerb weight: 1,371kg (3,020lb)
Fuel: 120l (26.4gal/31.7US gal)
Suspension: A-arms, coil springs, shock absorbers and anti-roll bars front and rear
Brakes: hydraulic; discs front and rear
Compression ratio: 10.5 : 1

The Countach was first shown at the Geneva Motor Show in 1971; it caused a instant sensation then, and continues to do so today. Styled by Marcello Gandini at Bertone, it had hinged doors which opened vertically from one pivot and a very shallow windscreen angle which formed a continuation of the bonnet line. The original prototype car shown at Geneva had a much cleaner line, lacking the complicated detail which creates the interesting visual distinction of the production cars.

Other features of this sharp-edged expression of the designer's art are the daring shape of the rear wheel arches, in direct contrast to the front round arches, and the rear wing which was an optional

extra, although the Countach just does not look complete without it.

The Countach was finally ready in March 1974, and gradually became better and better, partly in competition with Ferrari to produce the fastest supercar.

The Countach stayed in production with model upgrades to the LP500 with 4,754cc (290cu in) in 1982. Again, when Ferrari launched the Testarossa, Lamborghini countered with the next-generation Countach, the *quattrovalvole* LP500S in 1985 with a 5,167cc (315cu in) unit which gave 335kW (455bhp) and 0–97km/h (60mph) in a very fast 4.8sec. It was replaced by the Diablo in 1990.

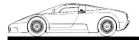

TRIUMPH TR7

Country of origin: UK
Date: 1975
Engine: inline 4-cylinder ohv with twin carburettors, producing 78.3kW (105bhp) at 5,500rpm
Transmission: 4-speed manual
Wheels driven: rear
Capacity: 1,998cc (121.9cu in)
Bore & stroke: 90.3 x 78mm (3.6 x 3.1in)
Performance: maximum speed 177km/h (110mph); 0–96.5km/h (60mph) in 9.1 seconds
Dimensions: wheelbase 2.159m (7ft 1in); length 4.173m (13ft 8.3in); width 1.681m (5ft 6.2in); height 1.267m (4ft 1.9in); track 1.410m (4ft 7.5in) front, 1.405m (4ft 7.3in) rear
Steering: rack and pinion
Kerb weight: 966kg (2,128lb)
Fuel: 54.6l (12gal/14.4US gal)
Suspension: coil springs and MacPherson struts with a live rear axle
Brakes: servo-assisted discs front, drums rear
Compression ratio: 9.2 : 1

British Leyland grew fast during the 1960s, and by 1968 the Group comprised the marques of Leyland; Standard; Triumph; Rover, including Land Rover; Morris, including MG; Wolseley; Riley; Austin, including Austin-Healey; Vanden Plas; Jaguar; Daimler, and Lancaster. In this way, the producers of Triumph's largest rival to its successful TR series, MG, had become its sibling.

The unitised coupé that emerged in 1975 was the TR7. It was completely different to the TR6, with a beam rear axle making full use of the BL parts bin. It handled better than any other previous TR model, was about as fast as the TR6 which it replaced, and was certainly more practical.

Unfortunately there were also many minus points; its oddball styling, and the indifferent build quality control from a new plant where poor industrial relations had tarnished its reputation, prevented the TR7 sales expectations from being realised, especially in North America.

PORSCHE 924

Country of origin: Germany
Date: 1976
Engine: front-mounted water-cooled sohc inline 4-cylinder producing 93.2kW (125bhp) at 5,800rpm
Transmission: 4-speed manual
Wheels driven: rear
Capacity: 1,984cc (121cu in)
Bore & stroke: 86.5 x 84.4mm (3.4 x 3.33in)
Performance: maximum speed 178.6km/h (111mph); 0–96.5km/h (60mph) in 11.9 seconds
Dimensions: wheelbase 2.4m (7ft 10.5in); length 4.321m (14ft 2.1in); width 1.684m (5ft 6.3in); height 1.27m (4ft 2in); track 1.42m (4ft 7.9in) front, 1.372m (4ft 6in) rear
Kerb weight: 1,096kg (2,415lb)
Fuel: 62.1l (13.6gal/16.4US gal)
Suspension: MacPherson struts and coil springs front; trailing arms and transverse torsion bars rear
Brakes: front discs, rear drums
Compression ratio: 8 : 1

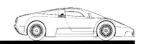

The first front-engine, water-cooled Porsche to go into production, the 924 relied heavily on VW and Audi parts – not surprisingly, as they had commissioned its design. However, the decision to market the model as a Porsche was made only late during its development.

With a 254mm (10in) longer wheel-base than the 911, the 924 was a 2+2 coupé which for Porsche broke new styling frontiers, with its sleek rounded contours dominated by a large compound curved rear window. The engine was a 2-litre designed by VW for use in the Type LT van and built by Audi, which also built the 924 in what had once been the old NSU factory at Neckarsulm.

Three-speed automatic transmission was offered as an option from 1976, and the new Getrag five-speed manual optional from 1978 became standard in the following year.

The 924 Turbo was launched in 1978, and the 924S model of 1988 was then the fastest of the series.

PORSCHE 928

Country of origin: Germany
Date: 1977
Engine: front-mounted water-cooled sohc inline V8 producing 222kW (300bhp) at 5,900rpm
Transmission: 5-speed manual
Wheels driven: rear
Capacity: 4,474cc (273cu in)
Bore & stroke: 95 x 78.9mm (3.7 x 3.1in)
Performance: maximum speed 230km/h (143mph); 0–96.5km/h (60mph) in 7.5 seconds
Dimensions: wheelbase 2.5m (8ft 2.4in); length 4.445m (14ft 7in); width 1.835m (6ft 0.2in); height 1.315m (4ft 3.8in); track 1.545m (5ft 0.8in) front, 1.515m (4ft 11.6in) rear
Kerb weight: 1,520kg (3,344lb)
Fuel: 86.9l (19.1gal/23US gal)
Suspension: upper and lower wishbones with coil springs front; independent with coil springs rear; anti-roll bars front and rear
Brakes: discs, front and rear
Compression ratio: 8.5 : 1

The 928 oozed comfort and was technically a masterpiece of motoring efficiency, reliability and build quality. Aerodynamically it was a match for anything, but the model just did not make the jaw drop. it lacked charisma; there was no pzazz.

At its heart was a V8 engine turned at 90 degrees with Bosch K-Jetronic fuel injection. A Daimler-Benz three-speed automatic was a transmission option which became standard in later series models. The complicated coil suspension had double wishbones at the front and an upper lateral arm and lower trailing arm per side at the rear.

The Series 2 model arrived in 1984, with anti-lock ventilated disc brakes and a top speed of 240km/h (149mph); 0–96.5km/h (60mph) was reduced to 6.5 seconds. The 5-litre engine was available from 1986 in the Series 4 model, which had a larger rear spoiler and revised nose section.

Below left: *a Triumph TR7 and* **below,** *a Porsche 924*

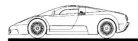

MAZDA RX-7

Country of origin: Japan
Date: 1978
Engine: 2-rotor Wankel producing 74.6kW (100bhp) at 6,000rpm
Transmission: 4-speed manual
Wheels driven: rear
Capacity: 1,146cc (69.9cu in) per rotor
Performance: maximum speed 196.3km/h (122mph); 0–96.5km/h (60mph) in 9.2 seconds
Dimensions: wheelbase 2.421m (7ft 11.3in); length 4.285m (14ft 0.7in); width 1.674m (5ft 5.9in); height 1.26m (4ft 1.6in); track 1.42m (4ft 7.9in) front, 1.4m (4ft 7.1in) rear
Steering: recirculating ball
Kerb weight: 1,098kg (2,420lb)
Fuel: 54.9l (12.1gal/14.5US gal)
Suspension: MacPherson struts, lower lateral links, coil springs, tubular shock absorbers and anti-roll bar front; live axle on lower trailing links, coil springs and anti-roll bar rear
Brakes: discs front, drums rear
Compression ratio: 9.4 : 1

Founded in 1920, Mazda began producing motorcycles in 1931, and then three-wheeled vehicles. After the Second World War production of trucks began in 1945, and in 1968 the first Mazda car was produced.

Mazda signed an agreement with NSU to produce the Wankel engine in 1961. It was used in the 110S coupé, the company's first sports car, in 1967. This was a front-engined car with the equivalent to a normal capacity of 1,964cc (119.8cu in) and a top speed of 185km/h (115mph). There was a gap between the end of production of the 110S in 1972, and the appearance of the RX-7 in 1978.

The RX-7 used a twin-rotor Wankel

engine and the first model, which remained in production until 1985, sold in excess of 500,000 units.

The model was restyled in 1986, and then looked more like a Porsche 924. The chassis was all new, having rack and pinion steering, MacPherson strut front suspension and a larger engine with a nominal capacity of 2,616cc (159.5cu in) which in normally-aspirated form gave 109.7kW (147bhp). The Turbo II turbocharged version was also available, which produced 135kW (182bhp).

Unfortunately, this second-generation RX-7 proved not nearly so popular; it was heavier, less responsive and the original competitive price of the 1978 model was no longer a factor.

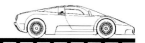

BMW M1

Country of origin: Germany
Date: 1979
Engine: mid-mounted dohc inline 6-cylinder with 4 valves per cylinder and fuel injection, producing 175.2kW (235bhp) at 6,500rpm
Transmission: 5-speed manual
Wheels driven: rear
Capacity: 3,453cc (210.7cu in)
Bore & stroke: 93.4 x 84mm (3.7 x 3.3in)
Performance: maximum speed 251km/h (156mph); 0–96.5km/h (60mph) 6.2 seconds
Dimensions: wheelbase 2.56m (8ft 4.8in); length 4.437m (14ft 6.7in); width 1.824m (5ft 11.8in); height 1.14m (3ft 8.9in); track 1.549m (5ft 1in) front, 1.575m (5ft 2in) rear
Steering: rack and pinion
Kerb weight: 1,509kg (3,325lb)
Fuel: 115.8l (25.5gal/30.6US gal)
Suspension: independent coil springs and double wishbones front and rear
Brakes: discs front and rear
Compression ratio: 9 : 1

Some 20 years after ending production of the 507, and a decade after its groundbreaking turbocharged 2002, BMW came back with what was intended to be an out and out racer. However, company policy changed and the M1 was never produced in sufficiently large quantities for it to be homologated in the right race category. Its racing history is not exciting therefore, but as a street car it was quite a different proposition, powered by BMW's 3.5-litre straight-six engine, which was mounted longitudinally amidships behind the passenger compartment in a space-frame. The styling was by Giugiaro and rendered in

fibreglass with both the steel frames and fibreglass bodies being made by Italdesign in Turin. Baur of Stuttgart fitted the engines and finished the cars.

It was an expensive diversification for BMW; the short run of only 456 examples made had been planned for production by Lamborghini, but that company was unable to proceed. The M1, however, with its power raised to 361.7kW (485bhp), became an important Pro-Car competitor in the series of curtain-raisers to grand prix races in 1979, when identical M1s were raced by Formula One drivers to entertain the crowds after qualifying on Saturdays. Today, they have become a valued collector's car.

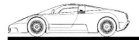

DE LOREAN DMC-2

Country of origin: UK
Date: 1981
Engine: V6 ohv with fuel injection, producing 96.9kW (130bhp) at 5,500rpm
Transmission: 5-speed manual
Wheels driven: rear
Capacity: 2,849cc (173.8cu in)
Bore & stroke: 91 x 73mm (3.6 x 2.9in)
Performance: maximum speed 175.4km/h (109mph); 0–96.5km/h (60mph) in 10.5 seconds
Dimensions: wheelbase 2.408m (8ft 0.8in); length 4.267m (14ft); width 1.989m (6ft 6.3in); height 1.14m (3ft 8.9in); track 1.59m (5ft 2.6in) front, 1.588m (5ft 2.5in) rear
Steering: rack and pinion
Kerb weight: 1,289kg (2,840lb)
Fuel: 51.1l (11.2gal/13.5US gal)
Suspension: coil springs front and rear
Brakes: discs front and rear
Compression ratio: 8.8 : 1

De Lorean's V6 engine was sourced from Volvo, with Bosch K-Jetronic fuel injection. The interior was leather-clad

This mid-engined coupé was built in Belfast, as the result of official efforts to help to create jobs in Northern Ireland, despite the fact that the area had no tradition of car building. The company was dependent for financial backing on the British government, and the car itself was the brainchild of John Z. De Lorean. It was promoted as an exclusive sports car, although in order to make sense financially it would have had to have outsold every other car in its category.

It was a controversial design, particularly the unpainted stainless-steel body panels, which easily gathered fingerprints. The plastic body structure itself was bolted directly onto a full-length backbone frame. In essence, the DMC-2

was full of gimmicks which extended even to gull-wing doors and custom-made spoked alloy wheels that were larger at the back than the front. The

gull-wing doors were each supported by a single gas strut. They were crammed with electronics, including the stereo speakers which made them far too heavy, and as a result they never worked properly and were apt to leak.

Production of the model totalled 8,583 between 1980 and 1981, although it is uncertain where all these went, or even if they were completed.

The manufacture and finish of the cars was a disgrace, the problems encountered by the purchasers being too many to list here. The government had no alternative but to put the company into receivership with debts

of £25m in October 1982, putting an end to a sorry car that failed to match its projected price, fuel economy or build quality.

FERRARI 512 BBi

Country of origin: Italy
Date: 1981
Engine: rear-mounted flat dohc 12-cylinder with 4 carburettors, producing 268.4kW (360bhp) at 6,200rpm
Transmission: 5-speed manual
Wheels driven: rear
Capacity: 4,942cc (301.6cu in)
Bore & stroke: 82 x 78mm (3.23 x 3.07in)
Performance: maximum speed 301km/h (188mph); 0–161km/h (100mph) in 10 seconds
Dimensions: wheelbase 2.499m (8ft 2.4in); length 4.361m (14ft 3.7in); width 1.801m (5ft 10.9in); height 1.12m (3ft 8.1in); track 1.501m (4ft 11.1in) front, 1.563m (5ft 1.5in) rear
Steering: rack and pinion
Kerb weight: 1,552kg (3,420lb)
Fuel: 120l (26.4gal/31.7US gal)
Suspension: independent double wishbones and coil springs front and rear
Brakes: power-assisted discs
Compression ratio: 9.2 : 1

Ferrari's first production mid-engined 12-cylinder car was the 365 GT4 Berlinetta Boxer (BB), also called the Boxer (*bottom picture*) . The BB designation refers to the flat-twelve engine, in which the pistons move away from each other, like boxers sparring. Ferrari had already used this configuration for some racing engines, but this was the first Ferrari road car that did not have a Vee engine.

It had a body of aluminium, steel and fibreglass and was launched in 1971, with production beginning in 1973. Fewer than 400 of the 365 GT4 were built before it gave way to the 512 BB in 1977. The latter's bigger engine was used to counteract more stringent exhaust emission laws, and in order to preserve performance the bore and stroke were increased. This raised the displacement from 4,390cc (267.9cu in) to 4,942cc (301.6cu in).

The 512 (*right*) also had a bib spoiler at the front and a single duct in front of each rear arch in order to cool the brakes. Other improvements embodied in the 512 included better seats and air conditioning.

The last significant change to the 512 was in 1981, when even tighter emission controls forced the retirement of the bank of Webers in favour of fuel injection. The model was still being manufactured until 1985, and production figures were respectively 387 and 1,936 for the 365 GT4BB and the 512 BB and BBi together.

The successor to the Boxer was introduced in 1984, and immediately assumed the mantle of Ferrari's flagship; it was the Testarossa.

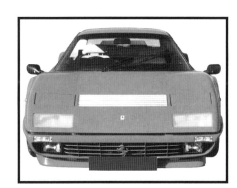

PORSCHE 944

Country of origin: Germany
Date: 1982
Engine: water-cooled sohc inline 4-cylinder, producing 106.6kW (143bhp) at 5,500rpm
Gears: 5-speed manual only
Wheels driven: rear
Capacity: 2,479cc (151.2cu in)
Bore & stroke: 100 x 78.9mm (3.9 x 3.1in)
Performance: maximum speed 212.4km/h (132mph); 0–96.5km/h (60mph) in 8.3 seconds
Dimensions: wheelbase 2.4m (7ft 10.5in); length 4.318m (14ft 2in); width 1.735m (5ft 8.3in); height 1.275m (4ft 2.2in); track 1.478m (4ft 10.2in) front, 1.45m (4ft 9.1in) rear
Steering: rack and pinion
Kerb weight: 1,266kg (2,790lb)
Fuel: 62.1l (13.6gal/16.4US gal)
Suspension: coil springs front, torsion bar rear
Brakes: discs front and rear
Compression ratio: 9.5 : 1

The first front-engined Porsches, the 944 and 924 were also the first to be water-cooled. They were also sharing some commonality with VW models, with the front suspension being similar to the VW Golf's, and the brakes coming from the K70.

The 944 is easily recognisable as the descendant of the 924, although it had evolved into a faster, better handling and more comfortable model. It featured a new impact-absorbing nose treatment and wide wheel arches.

Another advantage it had over the 924 was that it did not rely on the Audi LT70 van engine, but had a new four-cylinder designed by Porsche and derived from the 928's V8.

Porsche introduced the 944 Lux in the Spring of 1982, with a 121.5kW (163bhp) rated engine, which offered 200km/h (137mph) as its top speed. The Lux also had a three-speed automatic gearbox as an option.

Both the 944S with its dohc 4-valve engine rated at 140.1kW (188bhp) and the 944 Turbo were announced in 1985. The latter originally had a 2.5-litre (151.2cu in) sohc with a KKK turbocharger which increased its power to 161.8kW (217bhp).

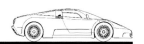

AUDI SPORT QUATTRO

Country of origin: Germany
Date: 1983
Engine: turbo-charged twin-cam inline 5-cylinder ohv with fuel injection, producing 228.2kW (306bhp) at 6,700rpm
Transmission: 5-speed manual
Wheels driven: 4-wheel drive
Capacity: 2,134cc (130.2cu in)
Bore & stroke: 79.3 x 86.4mm (3.1 x 3.4in)
Performance: maximum speed 249.4km/h (155mph); 0–96.5km/h (60mph) 4.8 seconds
Dimensions: wheelbase 2.223m (7ft 3.5in); length 4.161m (13ft 7.8in); width 1.781m (5ft 10.1in); height 1.344m (4ft 6.9in); track 1.486m (4ft 10.5in) front, 1.483m (4ft 10.4in) rear
Steering: rack and pinion
Kerb weight: 1,274kg (2,807lb)
Fuel: 90.1l (19.8gal/23.8US gal)
Suspension: coil springs front and rear
Brakes: discs front and rear
Compression ratio: 8 : 1

The Audi Quattro revolutionised the rally world in the 1980s, with its outstanding four-wheel drive and a 5-cylinder turbocharged engine that produced over 223.7kW (300bhp) and a lightning turn of speed.

The Quattro made its assault on the rally scene in October 1980 after its launch at the Geneva Motor Show in March of that year, but the Sport Quattro did not appear until September 1983. It looked quite normal on the exterior, but underneath was a different matter. The floorpan had lost 317mm (12.5 inches) from behind the front seats; the engine had a 50 per cent power boost from an alloy block and the body was lightened

by the use of Kevlar and fibreglass. The Sport was 272kg (600lb) lighter than the production cars.

The suspension was lowered and stiffened for 1984, the wheels were wider and ABS was included. The Quattro had been developed from the Audi 80, and initially the high price tag and performance were certainly not matched by cockpit comfort, layout or instrumentation; but as the Quattro developed, so trim and equipment improved. The changes demanded by rallying to the styling created obvious differences, but the Sport Quattro remained unequivocally a Quattro, a four-wheel drive marvel.

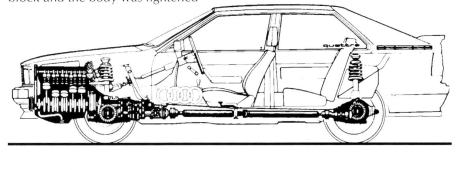

FERRARI TESTAROSSA

Country of origin: Italy
Date: 1984
Engine: dohc flat 12-cylinder with Bosch K-Jetronic fuel injection, producing 290.7kW (390bhp) at 6,800rpm
Transmission: 5-speed manual
Wheels driven: rear
Capacity: 4,9431cc (301.5cu in)
Bore & stroke: 82 x 78mm (3.22 x 3.07in)
Performance: maximum speed 286km/h (178mph); 0–96.5km/h (60mph) 5.3 seconds
Dimensions: wheelbase 2.55m (8ft 4.4in); length 4.486m (14ft 8.6in); width 1.976m (6ft 5.8in); height 1.13m (3ft 8.5in); track 1.519m (4ft 11.8in) front, 1.661m (5ft 5.4in) rear
Steering: rack and pinion
Kerb weight: 1,661kg (3,660lb)
Fuel: 104.8l (23gal/27.7US gal)
Suspension: independent upper and lower transverse wishbones and coil springs front and rear
Brakes: discs front and rear
Compression ratio: 8.8 : 1

The Testarossa ('red head') assumed the mantle of Ferrari's flagship when the name was resurrected in 1984.

It had a larger and more comfortable cockpit than the Berlinetta Boxer, which it replaced. The wide and low wedge shape was evolved in a wind tunnel, with a special attention being paid to aerodynamic downforce. It was designed specifically for auto-route use, with styling by Pininfarina. The Testarossa's transversely mid-mounted engine was served by a pair of radiators installed to the aft of the passenger compartment, in the flanks, just ahead of the rear wheels. The large egg-slicer side grilles also resulted from the wind tunnel tests, and improved cooling efficiency to the rear-mounted radiator. They were very necessary, for the engine was much more powerful than the Boxer's.

The Testarossa was a civilised and practical supercar. Its big performance gain was the result of modern 4-valve technology, which enabled it to reach 0–161km/h (100mph) in 11.2 seconds. It was a car that was happy when pushed to its limits, but in vying with Lamborghini, the Testarossa was forced to conceed its 0–96.5km/h (60mph) speed to the Countach. It was, however, more user-friendly on the road.

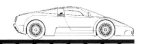

PONTIAC FIERO GT

Country of origin: USA
Date: 1984
Engine: transversely mid-mounted sohc inline 4-cylinder with fuel injection, producing 68.6kW (92bhp) at 4,000rpm
Gears: 4-speed manual
Wheels driven: rear
Capacity: 2,471cc (150.8cu in)
Performance: maximum speed 165.7km/h (103mph) 0–96.5km/h (60mph) in 10.9 seconds
Dimensions: wheelbase 2.372m (7ft 9.4in); length 4.072m (13ft 4.3in); width 1.75m (5ft 8.9in); height 1.191m (3ft 10.9in); track 1.468m (4ft 9.8in) front, 1.491m (4ft 10.7in) rear
Steering: rack and pinion
Kerb weight: 1,184kg (2,610lb)
Fuel: 36.6l (8.5gal/10.2US gal)
Suspension: upper and lower A-arms and coil springs front and rear
Brakes: discs front and rear
Compression ratio: 9 : 1

Pontiac was created in 1926 as a separate division of General Motors, and came to the fore in the 1960s under the guiding hand of John Z. De Lorean with a series of muscle cars.

Thus in 1984, when the Fiero was unveiled, it came from a producer without a real sports-car tradition. Unfortunately much of the Fiero came from other GM models and the public was soon to realise what was on offer – namely, an outdated pushrod ohv engine, front suspension and steering from the Chevrolet Chevette and rear suspension from GM's X-cars.

Much of Pontiac's camouflage could have been forgiven, but the Fiero's performance was found wanting, and all of this was reflected in the sales figures, which dropped from over 135,000 in the first year of production to 45,000 in the second.

Pontiac tried to put things right by offering a 2,837cc (173.1cu in) V6 from 1984, a fastback-bodied GT in 1985 and a five-speed gearbox in 1986. The axe fell on the Fiero in 1988, when only 25,000 cars were produced and a series of engine fires in 1984 models had eventually led to a massive recall.

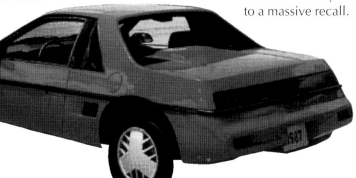

FERRARI 328GTB

Country of origin: Italy
Date: 1985
Engine: dohc V8 with 4 valves per cylinder and twin carburettors producing 193.9kW (260bhp) at 7,000rpm
Transmission: 5-speed manual
Wheels driven: rear
Capacity: 3,185cc (194.3cu in)
Bore & stroke: 83 x 73.6mm (3.3 x 2.9in)
Performance: maximum speed 249.4km/h (155mph), 0 to 96.5km/h (60mph) 6.6 seconds
Dimensions: wheelbase 2.35m (7ft 8.5in); length 4.295m (14ft 1.1in); width 1.72m (5ft 7.7in); height 1.12m (3ft 8.1in); track 1.473m (4ft 10in) front, 1.468m (4ft 9.8in) rear
Steering: rack and pinion
Kerb weight: 1,425kg (3,140lb)
Fuel: 51.5 litres (11.3gal/13.6 US gal)
Suspension: independent double wishbones and coil springs front; independent double wishbones, coil springs rear
Brakes: ventilated discs front and rear

The magnificent mass-produced 308s and 328s are among the most sophisticated road vehicles ever to wear the prancing horse badge. Furthermore, they have proved successfully that Maranello can produce practical machines for daily driving rather than Ferrari's earlier tradition of race-bred street cars. However, these 'Fiat-Ferraris' have surely lost some of the reflected glory of the earlier cars.

The Pininfarina-designed 308GTB was launched in 1975, and was succeeded by the 308i in 1981. The 308i had the more efficient fuel-injected engine that had first appeared in the Mondial. Paradoxically this had the effect of limiting the power immediately available through the

throttle, weakening the mid-range ability of the model, and putting 240km/h (150mph) out of reach. The 1982 *quattrovalvole* 'clean' engine hiked power to 180kW (240bhp), boosted torque, and restored the 308i's performance.

Ferrari introduced the transversely mid-mounted 3.2-litre 90-degree V8 in 1985 into the 308 body to provide a much-needed increase in power to 193.9kW (260bhp), and create the 328.

By the time the 308 series was replaced in 1988 it had become easily the most popular model in Ferrari's history, with production of the 328GTB alone at about 1800 units per year.

BMW Z1

Country of origin: Germany
Date: 1986
Engine: inline 6-cylinder ohv with fuel injection, producing 126.8kW (171bhp) at 5,800rpm
Transmission: 5-speed manual
Wheels driven: rear
Capacity: 2,494cc (152cu in)
Bore & stroke: 84 x 75mm (3.3 x 2.9in)
Performance: maximum speed 223.7km/h (139mph); 0–96.5km/h (60mph) 7.9 seconds
Dimensions: wheelbase 2.438m (8ft); length 3.924m (12ft 10.5in); width 1.701m (5ft 7in); height 1.244m (4ft 1in); track 1.422m (4ft 8in) front, 1.447m (4ft 9in) rear
Steering: power-assisted rack and pinion
Kerb weight: 1,337kg (2,944lb)
Fuel: 58.2.1l (12.8gal/15.4US gal)
Suspension: coil springs front and rear
Brakes: power-assisted; discs front, drums rear, with ABS
Compression ratio: 8.8 : 1

Built as a concept car, the Z1 was forced into production by public demand. The chassis was a steel and carbon composite monocoque covered by a fibreglass skin. The front suspension utilised MacPherson struts, while the rear suspension had BMW's Z-axle wishbone.

The Z1 was never destined to become a success. Sales reached only about 800 units by the time it was withdrawn from production in 1991, and the model was invariably considered to be overpriced; added to which, it never received any accolades from the motoring press, which criticised its steering, response, underpowered engine and poor value for money. This led to some garages putting additional power under the bonnet, and other personalised refinements were made; however, the Z1 still failed to attract, and even the gimmick of doors that slid down into the shell to afford access failed to catch the public's attention. Perhaps after all it was better that the Z1, that had been born without any design constraints as a rolling showcase for the BMW Technik division, was not further developed. This allowed

BMW's retro-styled Z3 model, launched in 1997, to come to the market as an altogether better car all round.

FERRARI MONDIAL 3.2

Country of origin: Italy
Date: 1986
Engine: dohc 90-degree V8 with 4
valves per cylinder, producing
193.9kW (260bhp) at 7,000rpm
Transmission: 5-speed manual
Wheels driven: rear
Capacity: 3,186cc (194.4cu in)
Bore & stroke: 83 x 73.6mm (3.27 x
3.9in)
Performance: maximum speed
233.3km/h (145mph); 0–96.5km/h
(60mph) in 7.1 seconds
Dimensions: wheelbase 2.649m (8ft
8.3in); length 4.641m (15ft 2.7in);
width 1.791m (6ft 0.5in); height
1.26m (4ft 1.6in); track 1.514m (4ft
11.6in) front, 1.534m (5ft 0.4in) rear
Steering: rack and pinion
Kerb weight: 1,609kg (3,545lb)
Fuel: 70l (15.4gal/18.5US gal)
Suspension: independent double wish-
bones and coil springs front and rear
Brakes: ventilated discs front and rear
Compression ratio: 9.2 : 1

The original Ferrari Mondial 8 was launched as a hard top coupé in March 1980 at the Geneva Motor Show, and as a convertible in 1983. The model is a 2+2, but mechanically is derived from the same family as the Ferrari Berlinettas, having centrally-placed rear engines and transverse axles. Its 8-cylinder 90-degree Vee engines went into production in 1974 with the Dino 308 GT4 3-litre engine. In 1975, the same engine was fitted to the two-seater 308GTB, and this was joined by the 208GTB.

A new version of the V8 engine was presented in 1982 as the Mondial Quattrovalvole, and in 1985 its capacity increased to 3.2 litres. The Mondial has created for itself a very clear-cut niche in the range, and Ferrari has responded by keeping the model up to date with important changes such as the longitudinal engine, new transverse clutch unit and electronic suspension for the launch of the Mondial t in 1989. The t indicates its transverse gear box.

The Mondial t is built on the classic tubular frame system, the rear part of which serves as the cradle for the engine. Pininfarina styled the body's softer lines and smaller rectangular side air vents in steel with the bonnet in aluminium. The nose was improved by the adoption of homofocal anti-glare headlights, and under the bonnet now resides the 3,405cc (207.8cu in) V8.

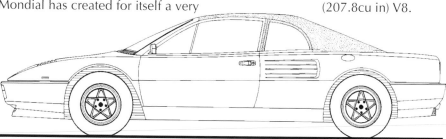

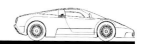

PORSCHE 959

Country of origin: Germany
Date: 1986
Engine: rear-mounted dohc flat
6-cylinder with dual turbochargers
and fuel injection, producing
335.5kW (450bhp) at 6,500rpm
Transmission: 6-speed manual
Wheels driven: 4-wheel drive
Capacity: 2,849cc (173.8cu in)
Bore & stroke: 95 x 67mm (3.7 x 2.6in)
Performance: maximum speed
323.4km/h (201mph); 0–96.5km/h
(60mph) in 4.7 seconds
Dimensions: wheelbase 2.299m (7ft
6.5in); length 4.26m (13ft 11.7in);
width 1.839m (6ft 0.4in); height
1.28m (4ft 2.4in); track 1.504m (4ft
11.2in) front, 1.549m (5ft 1in) rear
Kerb weight: 1,352kg (2,980lb)
Fuel: 90l (19.8gal/23.8US gal)
Suspension: upper and lower A-arms,
coil springs, dual tubular shock absorbers
and anti-roll bars front and rear
Brakes: anti-lock front and rear discs
Compression ratio: 8 : 1

Unveiled at the 1983 Frankfurt Motor
Show, the 959 was designed originally
as a competition car. However, Group
B competition, at which it had been
aimed, had been abandoned during
its development. Nonetheless Porsche
completed the planned 200-car
production run, converting them into
a limited-edition supercar which was
then probably the most technically
advanced road car ever built.

The 2.9-litre flat-six engine was
water-cooled, and four-wheel drive
was permanent, with a system that
employed sensors to vary the torque
split according to conditions.
With the contemporary
911 Carrera as its
basis, the 959

had the same wheelbase and a
similar central steel structure. A
bellypan covered its underside and
its ultra-wide tail was topped by a
large loop spoiler. The lower body of
the 959 was reshaped to improve its
aerodynamics, with ducts and vents
controlling the air flow through it to
reduce overheating.

Weight reduction was achieved by
rendering the doors and bonnet in
aluminium, the nose cap in poly-
urethene and the remainder in
fibreglass-reinforced Kevlar. Such was
the body shape that it achieved a
drag coefficient of 0.31 and, together
with zero lift, this made
the 959 extremely
stable at its top speed.

PORSCHE 968

Country of origin: Germany
Date: 1986
Engine: longitudinally-mounted dohc inline 4-cylinder with 4 valves per cylinder, producing 175kW (236bhp) at 6,200rpm
Transmission: 6-speed manual
Wheels driven: rear
Capacity: 2,990cc (182cu in)
Bore & stroke: 104 x 88mm (4.1 x 3.5in)
Performance: maximum speed 235km/h (146mph); 0–96.5km/h (60mph) in 6.4 seconds
Dimensions: wheelbase 2.4m (7ft 10.5in); length 4.32m (14ft 2.1in); width 1.73m (5ft 8.3in); height 1.27m (4ft 2.2in)
Steering: rack and pinion
Kerb weight: 1,403kg (3,086lb)
Fuel: 74l (16.3gal/19.6US gal)
Suspension: independent suspension front and rear
Brakes: vented brake discs with ABS
Compression ratio: 10.9 : 1

Porsche appeared to have mixed and matched when the company put together the 968: a bit of 928, a dash of 959, and a splash of 944 for good measure. In fact, only about 60 per cent of the 968 was borrowed, and most of those elements were welcome improvements over those in the 944, the model which it replaced.

The tail was roundish, rather like the 928's, and the pop-up headlights embedded in the bumpers were a real Porsche signature. Considering the model's pedigree, it came to the USA market at a very reasonable £35,000 ($44,500) base price and so proved to have been a worthwhile exercise.

The venerable 16-valve three-litre was stretched to provide 176kW (236bhp). This combined with the VarioCam system, which alters intake cam timing, increased torque at low revs and peak power at the top end.

On models sold in North America, the transmission was offered with an option of four-speed Tiptronic automatic. This was first seen on the 911 Carrera 2, but the manual with overdrive on both fifth and sixth is more suited to Europe's autoroutes.

There were many minor complaints about the build quality of the 968, especially the instrumentation and the effort necessary to unbolt the convertible top before the electric lowering process could be employed. The 968 has since evolved; its steering is more precise and the aerodynamics have improved the roadholding, but the 968 has a few more miles to go to become a supercar. However, it is undeniably now a better-handling and better-driving car than the original model.

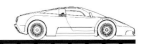

FERRARI F40

Country of origin: Italy
Date: 1988
Engine: longitudinally mid-mounted dohc 90-degree V8 with Weber Marelli fuel injection, producing 356.4kW (478bhp) at 7,000rpm
Transmission: 5-speed manual
Wheels driven: rear
Capacity: 2,936cc (179.1cu in)
Bore & stroke: 82 x 69.5mm (3.2 x 2.7in)
Performance: maximum speed 323.4km/h (201mph); 0–96.5km/h (60mph) in 4.5 seconds
Dimensions: wheelbase 2.451m (8ft 0.5in); length 4.43m (14ft 6.4in); width 1.981m (6ft 6in); height 1.13m (3ft 8.5in); track 1.595m (5ft 2.8in) front, 1.61m (5ft 3.4in) rear
Steering: rack and pinion
Kerb weight: 1,100kg (2,425lb)
Fuel: 119.6l (26.3gal/31.6US gal)
Suspension: independent double wishbones and coil springs front and rear
Brakes: discs front and rear
Compression ratio: 7.7 : 1

The F40 was built to celebrate 40 years of Ferrari cars, and to displace Porsche's 959 as the fastest production car in the world. What it lacked was the technical ingenuity of the Porsche, being more akin to the gut-wrenching screamers of the muscle car era. Indeed, Ferrari had purposely set out to evoke the memory of pre-Fiat days, when Ferrari customers bought the dream of driving machines that were virtually indistinguishable from the racing cars.

Its styling was by Pininfarina, with a high rear airfoil added akin to that of the Porsche 959 tail, and the wheels and tyres were of Indycar proportions. The outer panels and

floor are made of woven Kevlar and carbon fibre, providing both strength and lightness.

The whole car was put together in little over a year, from when Enzo Ferrari first made the proposal to an executive committee on 6 June 1986 to the press launch on 21 July the following year. The F40 had been developed into a street version of the GTO *Evoluzione*. Sadly, it was to be the last car that Enzo Ferrari presented, as the great man died on 14 August 1988. However, in the F40 he had achieved what he had always set out to do, to provide the thrill of driving a race car on the world's highways; so he left behind his own most fitting memorial.

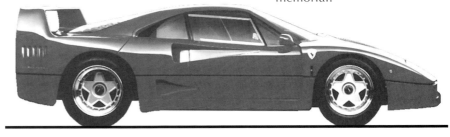

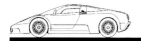

JAGUAR XJ220

Country of origin: UK
Date: 1988
Engine: mid-mounted quad-cam V6
24-valve twin Garrett T3 carburettors,
producing 401kW (542bhp) at 7,000rpm
Transmission: 5-speed manual
Wheels driven: 4-wheel drive
Capacity: 3,498cc (213.4cu in)
Bore & stroke: 94 x 84mm (3.7 x 3.3in)
Performance: maximum speed
335km/h (208mph); 0–96.5km/h
(60mph) in 3.8 seconds
Dimensions: wheelbase 2.64m (8ft
7.9in); length 4.93m (16ft 2.1in);
width 2m (6ft 6.7in); height 1.15m
(3ft 9.3in); track 1.709m (5ft 7.3in)
front, 1.588m (5ft 2.5in) rear
Steering: rack and pinion
Kerb weight: 1,470kg (3,241lb)
Fuel: 90l (19.8gal/23.8USgal)
Suspension: rocker arm-operated
Bilstein spring/damper units with
anti-roll bars front and rear
Brakes: discs front and rear with ABS
Compression ratio: 8.3 : 1

Proposed as a limited-production
supercar by a team of engineers
working under Jaguar's Jim Randle,
the XJ220 was hastily developed into
a prototype V12 supercar for the 1988
British Motor Show, following a long
gestation. It was rapturously received,
and Jaguar and TWR together formed
JaguarSport in 1989. This company,
headed by Tom Walkinshaw, was
convinced that the XJ220 project was
viable, but further development had
to wait for funds to be available until
after Ford's purchase of Jaguar.

After this, the first new car that Ford
sanctioned, in December 1989, was
the XJ220. JaguarSport redesigned the
car from the ground up, to offer a
production package of unmatched
performance, capable of beating the
world's best.

It was announced that up to 350
XJ220s would be built with 372.9kW
(500bhp) 24-valve V6 engines. Such
was the public reaction that this
planned production run completely
sold out within 48 hours.

The basic shape of the car had
remained unchanged for seven years:
by switching from the original and
basically XJR-12 V12 engine to the
V6, the wheelbase had been reduced
by some 203mm (8 inches) and the
overall length had also been shortened.

The V6 engine is cooled by a front-
mounted radiator, which is fitted at
an angle within the sloped nose, with
the large, long indentations in the
bottom of the doors leading to large
intercoolers, one on each side of the
engine.

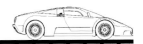

FERRARI 348 tb

Country of origin: Italy
Date: 1989
Engine: 90-degree V8 with fuel injection, producing 223.7kW (300bhp) at 7,000rpm
Transmission: 5-speed manual
Wheels driven: rear
Capacity: 3,405cc (207.7cu in)
Bore & stroke: 85 x 75mm (3.3 x 2.9in)
Performance: maximum speed 275.1km/h (171mph); 0–96.5km/h (60mph) in 6 seconds
Dimensions: wheelbase 2.451m (8ft 0.5in); length 4.234m (13ft 10.7in); width 1.895m (6ft 2.6in); height 1.171m (3ft 10.1in); track 1.504m (4ft 11.2in) front, 1.58m (5ft 2.2in) rear
Steering: rack and pinion
Kerb weight: 1,484kg (3,270lb)
Fuel: 87.6l (19.3gal/23.2US gal)
Suspension: coil springs front and rear
Brakes: power-assisted discs front and rear with ABS
Compression ratio: 10.4 : 1

At the end of the 1974 Formula One season, Ferrari presented the new 312T Formula One car, named for its three (cylinder capacity) twelve (number of cylinders) T (transversal), in which a conical transmission was placed at the entrance to the gear box, which in turn became transversal.

Ferrari launched the 348 tb along with the ts at the 1989 Frankfurt Motor Show, with the t again characterising the powerplant with a transversal gear box.

The 348 was an improvement on the 328GTB, which it replaced, but the 348 was started from scratch. Ferrari had rethought the general formulation of the model, from the sculptured line of the body right down to the power train.

Overall, the 348 is more compact and more aggressive-looking than the 328, partly because of the reduction of the rear overhang. The wheelbase is longer, which adds both to the internal comfort and to the stability on the straight, but loses nothing on the bends. The overall length is almost unchanged, however, which gives more emphasis to the front overhang, which has also remained unchanged.

The styling is again the work of Pininfarina. The tb is the berlinetta version, and the ts the spyder, with a removeable roof. Some stylistic features, notably the grating on the doors which direct air towards the rear air ducts, echo the Testarossa.

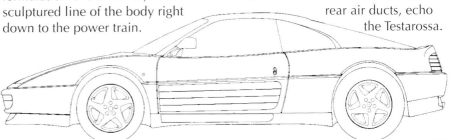

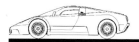

MITSUBISHI 3000 GT VR-4

Country of origin: Japan
Date: 1989
Engine: turbocharged V6 ohv with fuel injection, producing 223.7kW (300bhp) at 6,000rpm
Transmission: 5-speed manual
Wheels driven: 4-wheel drive
Capacity: 2,972cc (181.3cu in)
Bore & stroke: 91.1 x 76mm (3.6 x 3in)
Performance: maximum speed 255.8km/h (159mph); 0–96.5km/h (60mph) in 6.3 seconds
Dimensions: wheelbase 2.469m (8ft 1.2in); length 4.584m (15ft); width 1.839m (6ft 0.4in); height 1.285m (4ft 2.6in); track 1.56m (5ft 1.4in) front, 1.58m (5ft 2.2in) rear
Steering: power-assisted rack and pinion
Kerb weight: 1,759kg (3,875lb)
Fuel: 74.9l (16.5gal/19.8US gal)
Suspension: coil springs front and rear
Brakes: power-assisted discs front and rear with ABS
Compression ratio: 8 : 1

Mitsubishi was originally founded in 1870 as a shipping company; its first car was based on a Fiat design and appeared in 1917. Its first cars designed domestically did not appear until 1959, and early models all had engines of under 500cc (30.5cu in). The car division of what by now had become a huge corporation became independent in 1979, and Chrysler took a 35 per cent holding in it in 1981.

The company moved into the higher performance market with turbocharged engines which powered its saloons and the Eclipse coupé.

Mitsubishi announced its first sports car, the 3000 GT, in 1989 and it was available the following year.

Marketted in North America as the Dodge Stealth and in Japan as the Starion GTO, the 3000 GT has received worldwide acclaim as a state-of-the-art performance thoroughbred. It is a roomy 2+2 coupé with 4-wheel drive, 4-wheel steering, 4-wheel ABS braking, and 4-wheel electronically-controlled suspension. In 1997, a new 6-speed transmission was developed to maximise performance.

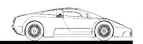

HONDA NSX

Country of origin: Japan
Date: 1990
Engine: dohc 60-degree V6 with 4 valves per cylinder and port fuel injection, producing 201.3kW (273bhp) at 7,100rpm
Transmission: 5-speed overdrive manual
Wheels driven: rear
Capacity: 2,977cc (182cu in)
Bore & stroke: 90 x 78mm (3.5 x 3.1in)
Performance: maximum speed 260.7km/h (162mph); 0–96.5km/h (60mph) in 5.8 seconds
Dimensions: wheelbase 2.53m (8ft 3.6in); length 4.404m (14ft 5.4in); width 1.811m (5ft 11.3in); height 1.171m (3ft 10.1in); track 1.509m (4ft 11.4in) front, 1.529m (5ft 0.2in) rear
Steering: rack and pinion
Kerb weight: 1,340kg (2,951lb)
Fuel: 70.1l (15.4gal/18.5US gal)
Suspension: upper and lower A-arms, coil springs front and rear
Brakes: discs front and rear with ABS
Compression ratio: 10.2 : 1

Since its launch in 1990, Honda's NSX two-seat fixed-head coupé has established itself as one of the world's greatest mid-engined sports cars. It is the first modern production car in which aluminium is used for the whole structure as well as the bodywork. This makes for an enhanced power-to-weight ratio, which together with its 3-litre dohc VTEC engine provides excellent acceleration.

By 1995, Honda had provided its supercar with its unique F-matic semi-automatic gearchange system that was developed from Formula One, and a 'drive-by-wire' electrically-actuated throttle to improve deceleration and control of the conventional traction control system. Larger wheels

and tyres had been introduced already, in 1994. The NSX-T open top was launched in 1995; this has a one-piece aluminium hard top which when removed can be stored under the glass panel of the rear window.

Both NSX models now feature electric power steering assistance, which was first introduced on the automatic option. The statistics which make the most interesting reading are Honda's fuel consumption claims for the NSX, which are: urban 7.26km/l (20.5mpg); at a constant 120km/h (75mph), 10.77km/l (30.4mpg) and for a constant 90km/h (56mph) a remarkable 12.8km/l (36.2mpg). A supercar without a thirst!

LAMBORGHINI DIABLO

Country of origin: Italy
Date: 1990
Engine: longitudinally mid-mounted
dohc V12, producing 361.7kW
(485bhp) at 7,000rpm
Transmission: 5-speed manual
Wheels driven: rear
Capacity: 5,707cc (348.2cu in)
Bore & stroke: 87 x 80mm (3.4 x
3.1in)
Performance: maximum speed
325km/h (202mph); 0–96.5km/h
(60mph) in 4.5 seconds
Dimensions: wheelbase 2.649m (8ft
8.3in); length 4.46m (14ft 7.6in);
width 2.04m (6ft 8.3in); height
1.105m (3ft 7.5in); track 1.509m (4ft
11.4in) front, 1.641m (5ft 4.6in) rear
Steering: rack and pinion
Kerb weight: 1,652kg (3,640lb)
Fuel: 99.9l (22gal/26.4US gal)
Suspension: independent coil springs
front and rear
Brakes: discs front and rear
Compression ratio: 10 : 1

Designed by Marcello Gandini and
launched in 1990, the Lamborghini
Diablo entered the supercar arena as
the world's fastest production car. The
body was honed by extensive wind
tunnel tests to create an exceptional
aerodynamic efficiency, yet without
the compromise of the rounded
shapes of many of its competitors.

As one has come to expect from
Lamborghini, the Diablo's appearance
is distinctly individual, with scissor-
action doors which reach up to the
heavens and an eye-catching rear wing.

The Diablo is the ultimate two-
seater, mid-engined sports car with
an engine derived from the legendary
Countach. It boasts a dramatic
performance to go with its looks. The
gearbox has been located ahead of

the engine and with the pricipal mass
located between the axles the weight
distribution is a near-perfect 51 : 49
ratio.

The VT version with active 4-wheel
drive has been added to the range,
together with a roadster which was
launched in December 1995. This
was the first Lamborghini roadster to
reach production. It was followed in
the Spring of 1996 by the Diablo SV
(for Sport Veloce), the quickest and
the most responsive road car that
Lamborghini has ever produced, with
that mystical blend of Italian supercar
charisma, exceptional performance
and total driver involvement.

One of the true exotics at the top of
the class, the Diablo is what dreams
are made of.

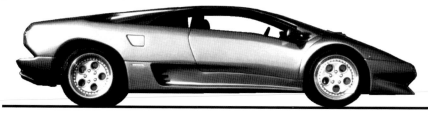

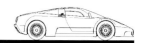

TVR GRIFFITH

Country of origin: UK
Date: 1990
Engine: V8 pushrod ohv, producing 208.8kW (280bhp) at 5,500rpm
Transmission: 5-speed manual
Wheels driven: rear
Capacity: 4,280cc (261.2cu in)
Bore & stroke: 94 x 77mm (3.7 x 3.03in)
Performance: maximum speed 259km/h (161mph); 0–96.5km/h (60mph) in 4.7 seconds
Dimensions: wheelbase 2.286m (7ft 6in); length 3.965m (13ft 0.1in); track 1.473m (4ft 10in) front, 1.483m (4ft 10.4in) rear
Steering: rack and pinion
Kerb weight: 1,045kg (2,304lb)
Suspension: independent unequal-length wishbones, concentric coil springs and anti-roll bar front; independent unequal-length wishbones and coil springs rear
Brakes: ventilated discs front, solid discs rear
Compression ratio: 10.8 : 1

First shown at the 1990 Birmingham Motor Show, and in production since 1992, the Griffith is probably the most important model in TVR's recent history. It has seized the imaginations of many of the world's car enthusiasts: for instance, when road tested by *Autocar and Motor* in 1992, the reviewer opined 'with the Griffith, TVR might just have rewritten the rulebook on sports cars for all time, just as Jaguar did with the E-Type more than 30 years ago'.

The Griffith has that classical blend of beauty and performance, and is now powered by the TVR Power V8, producing 252kW (340bhp).

This provides an improvement in performance over the original Rover power block, cutting the 0–96.5km/h (60mph) time to 4.1 seconds, although the top speed remains little in excess of 257.4km/h (160mph). From this little car with a big heart the thrill is in its lively agility in traffic, which is admirably matched by its superb handling and roadholding.

The Griffith is clean and uncluttered, with no discrete bumpers or protruding door handles, just its smooth fibre-glass skin drawn tightly over the tubular backbone chassis to form a compact sports sensation.

BUGATTI EB110 GT

Country of origin: Italy
Date: 1991
Engine: V12 with 5 valves per cylinder and fuel injection, producing 412kW (550bhp) at 8,000rpm
Transmission: 6-speed manual
Wheels driven: 4-wheel drive
Capacity: 3,498cc (213.6cu in)
Bore & stroke: 81 x 56.6mm (3.2 x 2.2in)
Performance: maximum speed 342km/h (212.5mph); 0–96.5km/h (60mph) in 3.4 seconds
Dimensions: wheelbase 2.55m (8ft 4.4in); length 4.4m (14ft 5.2in); width 1.99m (6ft 6.3in); height 1.114m (3ft 7.9in); track 1.54m (5ft 0.6in) front and rear
Kerb weight: 1,341kg (2,955lb)
Fuel: 120l (26.4gal/31.7US gal)
Suspension: double wishbones and pull-rod system front; double wishbones, double springs and dampers rear
Brakes: ventilated discs front and rear
Compression ratio: 7.5 : 1

Bugatti Automobile SpA was founded in 1987 in Módena, the veritable home of the supercar, by Artioli Romana; by 1990, the new engine had been bench-tested at 412kW (550bhp), ahead of the lavish launch party at the Paris show in 1991. Four years later, after having spent £120 million ($180), the company was declared bankrupt on 22 September 1995: but what of the EB110 GT?

It carried all of the credentials needed by a world-class supercar. It had grunt, in the form of an immensely powerful supercharged longitudinally mid-mounted V12 engine permanently driving all four wheels through the 6-speed gearbox, and it had stunning looks to go with it; and those of the trade press who were allowed to road-test the car, described the road-

holding as limpet-tight. The EB110 was to be the first model in the renaissance of the famous marque; indeed a big saloon, the EB112 was unveiled at Geneva in 1993.

The first production car was delivered in 1992, and in May of that year a test car was officially timed at a speed of 342km/h (212.5mph), a world record for a homologated production road car and a speed surpassed only by the EB110SS (for Sport Stradale), the model purchased by F1 racing champion Michael Schumacher.

The EB110 was a dream car; the total number produced is still not known and we can only fantasise as to what might have been on the drawing board, had that horrible necessity money been available.

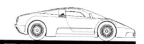

GINETTA G.33

Country of origin: UK
Date: 1991
Engine: front-mounted V8 with fuel injection, producing 149kW (200bhp) at 5,280rpm
Transmission: 5-speed manual
Wheels driven: rear
Capacity: 3,947cc (240.8cu in)
Bore & stroke: 94 x 71.1mm (3.7 x 2.8in)
Performance: maximum speed 233km/h (145mph); 0–96.5km/h (60mph) in 5 seconds
Dimensions: wheelbase 2.16m (7ft 1in); length 3.54m (11ft 7.6in); width 1.47m (4ft 9.8in); height 1.01m (3ft 3.9in)
Steering: rack and pinion
Kerb weight: 680kg (1,500lb)
Suspension: independent wishbone, coil springs and anti-roll bar front; independent lower wishbones, longitudinal links, coil springs and anti-roll bar rear
Brakes: ventilated discs front, solid discs rear

The Ginetta company was started by four Walklett brothers in 1958, and offered its first product, the G.2, as a kit car. By the 1960s, the company had progressed to almost fully-assembled cars, and emerged in the 1980s after difficult times with a new model, the mid-engined G.32.

During the intervening years, the company produced about 100 units of the G.2 kit car which was followed by the G.3. This was similar to the G.2, but with the body supplied almost complete. The G.4, G.5, G.6 and G.7 series

followed during the 1960s and sold about 500 units, and Ginetta's most successful model,

the G.15, came in 1968. This used Triumph Herald front suspension together with the Hillman Imp engine, transaxle and rear suspension. Its top speed was 153km/h (95mph). The G.21 was launched in 1970. This was a larger version of the G.15 and sold best as a fully-assembled car.

The G.27 made its début in 1985, and is best described as a multi-donor two-seater sports car, available separately as a starter kit or body kit, and from which the G.33 and G.40 have been developed and offered as fully assembled cars. These are no-compromise sports cars, aimed at the enthusiast who enjoys the brute power of open-air motoring.

PORSCHE 911 CARRERA RS

Country of origin: Germany
Date: 1991
Engine: rear-mounted ohc flat
6-cylinder with fuel injection, producing
193.9kW (260bhp) at 6,100rpm
Transmission: 5-speed manual
Wheels driven: rear
Capacity: 3,600cc (220cu in)
Bore & stroke: 100 x 76.4mm (3.9 x 3in)
Performance: maximum speed
259km/h (161mph); 0–96.5km/h
(60mph) in 4.9 seconds
Dimensions: wheelbase 2.271m (7ft
5.4in); length 4.25m (13ft 11.3in);
width 1.778m (5ft 10in); height
1.311m (4ft 3.6in); track 1.435m (4ft
8.5in) front, 1.494m (4ft 10.8in) rear
Steering: power-assisted rack and
pinion
Kerb weight: 1,195kg (2,632lb)
Fuel: 76.8l (16.9gal/20.3US gal)
Suspension: coil springs front and rear
Brakes: power-assisted discs front and
rear with ABS
Compression ratio: 11.3 : 1

Although the Carrera 4 was a true
911 in style it was 85% new, having
almost all new and more softly-
contoured, body panels; modified
suspension; power steering, and anti-
lock brakes. It was launched in
1989, with permanent 4-wheel drive
(31/69 per cent split) and a twin-plug
3.6-litre version of the flat-six engine.

A two-wheel drive version, the
Carrera 2, came out later in the same
year, and is fractionally quicker than
the 4-wheel drive 911. It was hailed
by the press as the best of the 911s
ever, but in 1991 the Carrera Turbo
made its début alongside the 911
Turbo, both being based on the
Carrera 2 chassis platform.

The Turbo has a fixed whale tail,
unlike the Carrera's retractable rear
spoiler, which creates more drag but
which works effectively to minimise

lift, and its base houses the intercooler.

There is a single KKK turbocharger,
which has a maximum boost of 0.7
bar and although the earlier turbos
had a four-speed gearbox to handle
the power, Porsche now fits a five-
speed which has proved more than
equal to the task.

The Porsche 911 was the first high-
performance car to be supercharged,
and has provided the model with
huge reserves of power which are
complemented by remarkable limits
of roadholding. This adds up to a
machine of startling performance,
matched by its reliability, fuel efficiency
and ease of driving.

Porsche's RS models are traditionally
featherweight racers, first introduced
in 1972. They were superbly balanced,
with fibreglass rear spoilers that
boosted maximum speed.

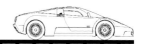

DODGE VIPER

Country of origin: USA
Date: 1992
Engine: 90-degree V10 ohv with fuel injection, producing 298.3kW (400bhp) at 5,500rpm
Transmission: 6-speed manual
Wheels driven: rear
Capacity: 7,989cc (487.4cu in)
Bore & stroke: 101.6 x 98.6mm (4 x 3.9in)
Performance: maximum speed 305.7km/h (190mph); 0–96.5km/h (60mph) in 4.1 seconds
Dimensions: wheelbase 2.443m (8ft 0.2in); length 4.369m (14ft 4in); width 1.92m (6ft 3.6in); height 1.173m (3ft 10.2in); track 1.514m (4ft 11.6in) front, 1.544m (5ft 0.4in) rear
Steering: rack and pinion
Kerb weight: 1,357.5kg (2,990lb)
Suspension: MacPherson struts, coil springs and anti-roll bar front and rear
Brakes: 330mm (13in) ventilated discs front and rear
Compression ratio: 9.1 : 1

The Dodge brothers made their first car in 1914, and quickly grew to be the second most popular American marque before becoming part of the Chryler Corporation in 1928.

After the Second World War, there was a long wait before a Dodge sports model eventually arrived as the Charger in 1968. However, it was not until the Stealth launch in 1990 that Dodge made the breakthrough. The Stealth sports coupé was a Mitsubishi 3000 in all but name, unsurprisingly as Dodge had been selling Mitsubishi models in North America since 1970.

Then came the Viper, planned for limited production. It oozed raw power, and was a frill-less, thrill-packed roadster.

The Viper GTS coupé was a star of the 1996 Le Mans 24-Hour race, after which Chrysler marketted a street version which combined all of the spine-tingling qualities of the awesome 8-litre V10 with the relative sophistication of an air-conditioned coupé.

With this additional comfort came additional equipment, but then the Viper team in Detroit had many more problems than just bolting a roof on the roadster. The end result was a coupé that was 90% new, with the body and interior being all new. The V10 engine was lightened and extensively modified to produce more power. The Viper body is made in several large pieces, fastened mechanically into a complete shell, with the bonnet section separating just above the headlamps and at the cowl.

MCLAREN F1

Country of origin: UK
Date: 1992
Engine: mid-mounted BMW quad chain-driven sohc 60-degree V12 with fuel injection, producing 410.4kW (550bhp) at 7,000rpm
Transmission: 6-speed manual
Wheels driven: rear
Capacity: 6,064cc (370cu in)
Bore & stroke: 86 x 87mm (3.39 x 3.4in)
Performance: maximum speed 322+km/h (200+mph); 0–96.5km/h (60mph) in 3.9 seconds
Dimensions: wheelbase 2.718m (8ft 11in); length 4.288m (14ft 0.8in); track 1.567m (5ft 1.7in) front, 1.473m (4ft 10in) rear
Steering: rack and pinion
Kerb weight: 1,018kg (2,244lb)
Suspension: double wishbones with horizontal coil springs and lightweight coaxial damper units operated by rocker arms front and rear
Brakes: Brembo iron discs front and rear
Compression ratio: 10.5 : 1

Set up by New Zealand racing driver Bruce McLaren shortly before his death in 1970, the company built its first supercar in 1969, the M6GT. It was a spinoff from the Can-Am M6B, with a monocoque construction designed by Robin Herd and Gordon Coppuck, with power provided by a Chevrolet V8.

Production of the M6GT was halted after McLaren's death, but a new company, McLaren International, announced the 2+1-seater F1 in 1990, and unveiled the stunning supercar at Monaco in 1992. In developing the F1, McLaren drew heavily on its immense Formula One experience to built what many *aficionados* consider the last word in supercar production.

The body is moulded in carbon composites, integrated with the chassis and finished with new-generation, environment-friendly coatings. There are carbon doors and sills to resist side impact, with racing-style skid plates beneath. Under heavy braking pressure, a foil rises automatically, putting pressure on the rear and cancelling any tendency to nose dive. The doors are of a beetle-wing design, and lift automatically when opened. This means that only the lower sections of the side windows are retractable. Furthermore, they cannot be opened at speeds in excess of 210km/h (130mph).

Whichever way you look at it, the F1 is *the* ultimate 'road car'.

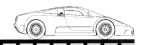

ASTON MARTIN DB7

Country of origin: UK
Date: 1993
Engine: supercharged dohc inline 6-cylinder with fuel injection, producing 250kW (335bhp) at 5,750rpm
Transmission: 5-speed manual
Wheels driven: rear
Capacity: 3,239cc (197.6cu in)
Performance: maximum speed 266km/h (165mph); 0–100km/h (62mph) in 5.7 seconds
Dimensions: wheelbase 2.591m (8ft 6in); length 4.631m (15ft 2.3in); width 1.82m (5ft 11.5in); height 1.268m (4ft 2in); track 1.524m (5ft) front, 1.53m (5ft 0.3in) rear
Steering: power-assisted rack and pinion
Kerb weight: 1,725kg (3,804lb)
Fuel: 89l (19.6gal/23.5USgal)
Suspension: independent double wishbones, coil springs and anti-roll bars front and rear
Brakes: ventilated discs front and rear with ABS
Compression ratio: 8.3 : 1

Introduced at the Geneva Motor Show in March 1993, the DB7 went into production at the beginning of 1994. The car was not launched on the North American market until the Detroit motor show in January 1996, where the Volante convertible model made its public début.

Production of the DB7 is running at about 700 units a year, a significant number considering that total Aston Martin production since 1913 is only about 13,500 units.

The DB series had halted in 1971, when the DB6 ceased production, but the DB7 continues the heritage the DB line established, being a front-engined, rear-wheel driven 2+2 sports car with the proportions and design themes of its forebears. It is amost exactly the same length as the DB6, but lower and wider in the modern idiom, and construction takes full advantage of the latest composite materials, technology and manufacturing techniques. The all-aluminium intercooled engine has been specially designed and developed for the DB7, with electronically-controlled sequential fuel injection linked to a three-way catalyst in the exhaust system.

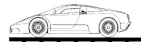

LISTER STORM

Country of origin: UK
Date: 1993
Engine: twin cam 60-degree V12 producing 485kW (655bhp) at 6,600rpm
Transmission: 5-speed manual
Wheels driven: rear
Capacity: 6,996cc (426.9cu in)
Bore & stroke: 94 x 84mm (3.7 x 3.3in)
Performance: maximum speed 322+km/h (200+mph); 0–96.5km/h (60mph) in 4.1 seconds
Dimensions: wheelbase 2.591m (8ft 6in); length 4.55m (14ft 11in); width 1.975m (6ft 5.75in); height 1.321m (4ft 4in); track 1.563m (5ft 1.5in) front, 1.93m (6ft 4in) rear
Steering: power-assisted rack and pinion
Kerb weight: 1,438kg (3,169lb)
Fuel: 100l (22gal/26.4USgal)
Suspension: unequal-length wishbones, coil springs, front; control arms and adjustable anti-roll bar, rear
Brakes: dual-circuit ventilated discs front and rear
Compression ratio: 12.5 : 1

The first Lister sports racer was designed in 1954 by Brian Lister, and in 1957 the Lister works Jaguar dominated the season, winning 11 out of 14 races. However, it was not until the 1980s that Lister returned to the sport, by developing its high-performance supercars based on the Jaguar XJ-S. Indeed, Lister has stayed loyal to Jaguar in that the V12 uses the Jaguar cylinder block and heads.

In 1991, design work started on the Lister Storm, which was launched in October 1993. It was the world's first full flat-bottomed front-engined car featuring underbody aerodynamics. Lister has succeeded in bringing together high-technology

engineering in developing this supercar, which because of having the V12 front-mounted (in fact so far back in the aluminium honeycomb monocoque that it would best be described as front to mid-engined) is also a true 2+2.

The layout provides an excellent 50 : 50 balance from front to rear, which provides the Storm with its very responsive and sure handling especially at high speed, when it provides a lower decibel level than any other 321.8km/h (200mph) car on the market at the beginning of the 1990s. The company went on to build a special racing version to compete in the 1995 Le Mans 24-Hour race.

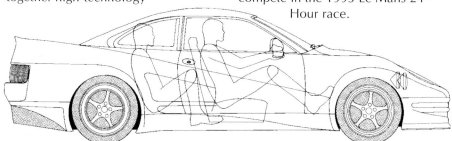

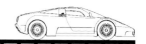

SPECTRE R42

Country of origin: UK
Date: 1993
Engine: mid-mounted V8, producing 259kW (350bhp) at 5,900rpm
Transmission: 5-speed manual
Wheels driven: rear
Capacity: 4,601cc (280.7cu in)
Bore & stroke: 90.2 x 90mm (3.55 x 3.54in)
Performance: maximum speed 285km/h (175mph); 0–96.5km/h (60mph) in 4.2 seconds
Dimensions: wheelbase 2.398m (8ft 1in); length 4.178m (13ft 8.5in); width 1.854m (6ft 1in); height 1.092m (3ft 7in); track 1.6m (5ft 3in) front, 1.549m (5ft 1in) rear
Steering: power-assisted rack and pinion
Kerb weight: 1,280kg (2,816lb)
Fuel: 40.9l (9gal/10.8US gal)
Suspension: double A-arms front; inverted A-arms, parallel radius rods rear; gas shock absorbers front and rear
Brakes: ventilated discs front and rear
Compression ratio: 9.85 : 1

The original concept was by G.T. Developments, which as the GTD42 progressed as far as a single running prototype. The project design was then developed by Spectre, which had Derek Bell as a director.

G.T. Developments produced copies of the Ford GT40 from the mid-1980s; the company also produced copies of the Lamborghini Countach and the Lola 170 Mk III, using V8s from either Chevrolet, Ford or Rover.

At the end of 1993, G.T. launched its first all-original design, a 223.7kW (300bhp) supercar intended as a contemporary roadgoing version of the Ford GT40, so named because it stood 1.01m (40in) tall. Similarly, the

R42's designation denoted a body just 51mm (2in) taller, although with Spectre it grew a further inch.

The R42 entered production powered by the V8 from Ford's Mustang Cobra. It had a breathtaking straight-line performance, comparable with other 1990s supercars of far more prestigious lineage. The R42 entered into GT racing with the ALCO Motorsport team in 1997, and also took the starring role in the motion picture *RPM*.

During 1997 unfortunately the Spectre company went into liquidation, only to reappear later in the year as Spectre Cars UK Ltd, unveiling the new Spectre R45 at the London Motor Show.

TVR CERBERA

Country of origin: UK
Date: 1993
Engine: 75-degree V8, producing 259kW (350bhp) at 6,500rpm
Transmission: 5-speed manual
Wheels driven: rear
Capacity: 4,185cc (255.4cu in)
Bore & stroke: 94 x 71mm (3.7 x 2.8in)
Performance: maximum speed 256.8km/h (160mph); 0–96.5km/h (60mph) in 4.2 seconds
Dimensions: wheelbase 2.566m (8ft 5in); length 4.28m (14ft 0.5in); width 1.865m (6ft 1.4in); height 1.22m (4ft 0in); track 1.464m (4ft 9.6in) front, 1.47m (4ft 9.8in) rear
Steering: rack and pinion
Kerb weight: 1,100kg (2,425lb)
Fuel: 65l (14.3gal/17.2US gal)
Suspension: multi-tubular steel frame backbone chassis with unequal-length wishbones, coil springs and anti-roll bars front and rear
Brakes: ventilated discs front and rear
Compression ratio: 9.8 : 1

The Cerbera was conceived as a styling exercise in the summer of 1993, when the design team sculpted the car out of full-size blocks of foam. Excited by the handsome grand tourer that began to take shape, TVR pushed ahead to prepare a prototype for the 1993 London Motor Show.

Originally designed to have a Rover engine, Cerbera production coincided with the development of TVR's own AJP8 powerplant, and the Cerbera became the first roadgoing TVR to feature the 4.2-litre (255.3cu in) block.

The AJP8 was developed out of a race engine, the result being that it features many elements more often found in an F1 engine

including a very sophisticated water circulation system, a lubrication system which delivers oil at high pressure to the engine and at low pressure to the crankshaft, and a block so rigid that it can be used as a stress member.

The AJP8 is an all-alloy engine with more torque in its various specifications than any other normally aspirated petrol engine of equivalent size and weight. In addition to its new engine, the model is a completely new car: new brakes, new chassis, new suspension and a different method of construction driven by public demand for a 2+2 TVR, the company's first since 1985.

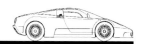

CATERHAM 21

Country of origin: UK
Date: 1994
Engine: dohc inline 4-cylinder with 4 valves per cylinder, producing 85kW (115bhp) at 6,000rpm
Transmission: 5-speed manual
Wheels driven: rear
Capacity: 1,588cc (96.9cu in)
Bore & stroke: 80 x 79mm (3.1 x 3.1in)
Performance: maximum speed 189km/h (118mph); 0–96.5km/h (60mph) in 6.4 seconds
Dimensions: wheelbase 2.23m (7ft 3.8in); length 3.8m (12ft 5.6in); width 1.58m (5ft 2.2in); height 1.06m (3ft 5.7in); track 1.32m (4ft 3.9in) front and rear
Kerb weight: 658kg (1,450lb)
Fuel: 66l (14.5gal/17.4US gal)
Suspension: double wishbones, coil springs, Bilstein dampers and anti-roll bar front; radius arms, progressive weight coil springs and dampers rear
Brakes: discs front and rear
Compression ratio: 10.5 : 1

Anniversary editions are not always a manufacturer's, best advertisement. However, Caterham's decision to mark 21 years of its manufacture of the Seven, which had been launched in 1957 by Lotus, is an overwhelming success. It replicates the Seven's performance, handling characteristics and compact dimensions, combined with the advantages of an all-new aerodynamic body style.

The 21 has a high-tech composite or traditionally lightweight aluminium bodywork, rigidly mounted onto its tubular spaceframe chassis, and utilises Rover's advanced all-alloy 16-valve K-series

powerplant. Two versions were available initially, the 1.6 or a 2-litre Supersport block, tuned to deliver 102kW (138bhp). The top speed for the Supersport was 210km/h (131mph) and the time from 0–96.5km/h (60mph) was 5.8 seconds.

The 21 maintains the Caterham tradition of small British sports car manufacture, that puts the driver's enjoyment first, second and always. In the 21, now Caterham has also produced a sports car that is as sleek and stylish in the cockpit as it is outside. Caterham introduced the new 1.8-litre Rover all-aluminium engine, that produces 140kW (189bhp) at 8,000rpm, in 1997.

FERRARI F50

Country of origin: Italy
Date: 1995
Engine: mid-mounted quad ohc 65-degree V12 driven by 2 Morse chains with Bosch Motronic injection, producing 382.6kW (513bhp) at 8,000rpm
Transmission: 6-speed manual
Wheels driven: rear
Capacity: 4,700cc (286.7cu in)
Bore & stroke: 85 x 69mm (3.35 x 2.72in)
Performance: maximum speed 325km/h (202mph); 0–161km/h (100mph) in 3.7 seconds
Dimensions: wheelbase 2.58m (8ft 5.6in); length 4.48m (14ft 8.4in); width 1.986m (6ft 6.2in); height 1.12m (3ft 8.1in); track 1.62m (5ft 3.8in) front, 1.602m (5ft 3.1in) rear
Steering: rack and pinion
Kerb weight: 1,230kg (2,712lb)
Fuel: 105l (23gal/27.6US gal)
Brakes: cast-iron Brembo discs splinted directly onto the aluminium hub
Compression ratio: 11.3 : 1

The F50 is the fruit of research based exclusively on Ferrari's vast experience in producing some 45 racing models and endless *gran turismo* and sports models. The F50 adopts the same constructional criteria as for an F1 car.

It is a mid-engined two-seater with a grand prix-derived V12 engine mounted as a structural unit directly onto the carbon-fibre honeycomb chassis. The engine also acts as a bearing structure for the gearbox-differential rear suspension assembly. The carbon-fibre monocoque encloses the aeronautical rubber-lined fuel tank, the pushrod suspension and separate-band braking system.

A direct descendant of Alain Prost's

1990 Formula One Ferrari, the F50 became the company's new flagship. Prost had driven the 3.5-litre 641/2 to six grand prix victories in that year, including Ferrari's one-hundredth, which was achieved at the French GP.

The F50 combines all the Formula One characteristics, slightly modified to give a two-seater with a larger and less powerful 4.7-litre engine, down from 559.4kW (750bhp) to 382.6kW (513bhp).

The car is deliberately devoid of luxury extras, and is available as either a berlinetta (coupé) or a barchetta (roadster). It is a supercar built exclusively for performance; passenger comfort takes a back seat.

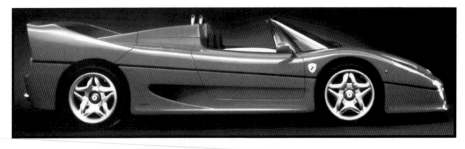

FERRARI F355 GTS

Country of origin: Italy
Date: 1995
Engine: quad ohc 90-degree V8 with 5 valves per cylinder, producing 280kW (380bhp) at 8,250rpm
Transmission: 6-speed manual
Wheels driven: rear
Capacity: 3,498cc (213.4cu in)
Bore & stroke: 85 x 77mm (3.35 x 3.03in)
Performance: maximum speed 295km/h (183mph); 0–96.5km/h (60mph) in 4.7 seconds
Dimensions: wheelbase 2.45m (8ft 0.5in); length 4.25m (13ft 11.3in); width 1.944m (6ft 4.5in); height 1.17m (3ft 10.1in); track 1.514m (4ft 11.6in) front, 1.615m (5ft 3.6in) rear
Steering: power-assisted rack and pinion
Kerb weight: 1,350kg (2,977lb)
Fuel: 88l (19.4gal/23.2US gal)
Suspension: unequal-length, non-parallel wishbones front and rear, with springs and anti-roll bars
Brakes: discs with cooling ducts
Compression ratio: 11 : 1

This Pininfarina design outperforms any previous Ferrari, and much of this achievement is in the designing of the body to the highest aerodynamic specification. The body design is the result of 1,300 hours of wind-tunnel analysis to ensure that cooling air flows meet the requirements of the power of the longitudinally mid/rear-mounted 8-cylinder normally aspirated engine.

The front bumper incorporates an air intake that cools the brake discs, while the spoiler area is shaped to optimise the air flow channelled forward but also into the underbody for negative lift. On the sides, the air ducts are generous but merge into the aerodynamically-shaped sills which

form part of the fairing of the 457mm (18-inch) wheels, an important element on a car set on wide-section tyres. At the rear, the wind tunnel experiments have produced a forceful tail profile which incorporates a spoiler to enhance grip.

The F355 is available as a two-seater berlinetta GTS with detachable aluminium and steel top, and an open-top spider. It is the first road car to incorporate a Formula One style gear-change, using two paddles mounted on the steering column. This enables a change to be made in just 0.125 seconds. The performance and style of the F355 are as exciting as anything to have come from Maranello.

BMW M ROADSTER

Country of origin: Germany
Date: 1996
Engine: twin-camshaft straight
6-cylinder with 4 valves per cylinder,
producing 236kW (321bhp) at
7,400rpm
Transmission: 5-speed manual
Wheels driven: rear
Capacity: 3,201cc (195.3cu in)
Bore & stroke: 86.4 x 91mm (3.4 x 3.6in)
Performance: maximum speed
250km/h (155mph); 0–100km/h
(62.15mph) in 5.4 seconds
Dimensions: wheelbase 2.459m (8ft
0.8in); length 4.025m (13ft 2.5in);
width 1.740m (5ft 8.5in); height
1.266m (4ft 1.8in); track 1.422m (4ft
8.0in) front, 1.492m (4ft 10.7in) rear
Steering: power-assisted rack and pinion
Kerb weight: 1,425kg (3,142lb)
Fuel: 51l (11.2gal/13.4USgal)
Suspension: spring strut axle front;
semi-trailing arms rear
Brakes: ventilated discs front and rear
Compression ratio: 11.3 : 1

The M (for Motorsport) designation defines those models developed by BMW's sports engineering arm, originally formed in 1972 as BMW Motorsport GmbH and from 1992 a reorganised subsidiary producing customer-tailored models, renamed BMW M GmbH. The M Roadster is its version of the Z3, with as much power packed into the chassis as it will comfortably accommodate; in this instance for Europe, a 24-valve 6-cylinder 3.2-litre unit which produces 74kW (100bhp) per litre.

Its acceleration is breathtaking, and the top speed is limited down to 250km/h (155mph). Externally, the design features more pronounced

front and rear bumpers and rear wheel arches and a new front apron; the rear view features four polished stainless-steel tail exhausts.

Other distinguishing features include white indicator lights and redesigned styling for the side air vents, door sills and 432mm (17-inch) light alloy wheels, of a unique design. Internally, the cockpit is furnished with leather sports seats and retro-style round analogue instruments and the steering wheel is a three-spoke design.

However, as we go to press the car awaits a special new engine for the USA before its launch there.

FERRARI 456 GT

Country of origin: Italy
Date: 1996
Engine: quad ohc 65-degree V12, producing 325kW (436bhp) at 6,250rpm
Transmission: 6-speed manual
Wheels driven: rear
Capacity: 5,473.9cc (334cu in)
Bore & stroke: 88 x 75mm (3.46 x 2.95in)
Performance: maximum speed 300km/h (186mph); 0–96.5km/h (60mph) in 5.1 seconds
Dimensions: wheelbase 2.6m (8ft 6.4in); length 4.73m (15ft 6in); width 1.92m (6ft 3.6in); height 1.3m (4ft 3.2in); track 1.585m (5ft 2.4in) front, 1.606m (5ft 3.2in) rear
Steering: power-assisted rack and pinion
Kerb weight: 1,690kg (3,726lb)
Fuel: 110l (24.2gal/29US gal)
Suspension: unequal-length non-parallel arms, helical coil springs and telescopic dampers with stabiliser bars both front and rear
Brakes: ventilated discs front and rear
Compression ratio: 10.6 : 1

There have been many four-seaters from the stable of the prancing horse, the first of which were designed by Vignale and Ghia, but undoubtedly the best were produced in collaboration with Pininfarina. The first Ferrari 2+2 coupé was the 250 of 1960, since when larger engines led to the 330 of 1964, the 365 of 1967, the 365 GT4 of 1972, the 400i automatic of 1976 (the first Ferrari to offer a choice of automatic or manual transmission), and then the 412 of 1985.

The Ferrari 456 GT 2+2 now follows this tradition with a special version, the 456 GTA, in which the A stands for automatic. In Ferrari's traditional main market of North America 2+2s are traditionally more frequently requested with automatic transmission. The 456 GT pre-sold 1,100 units two years before launch, compared to a total of 1,576 units of the 400 with mechanical gearbox sold in its entire 18-year life cycle, and 1,520 of the 400i automatic in 15 years.

Both of these current 456 models are powered by 5.5-litre longitudinally front-mounted engines with 4 valves per cylinder with Bosch Motronic fuel injection and 4 overhead camshafts. The transmission is also rear-mounted and a mobile wing built into the rear bumper which changes the angle according to the vehicle's speed.

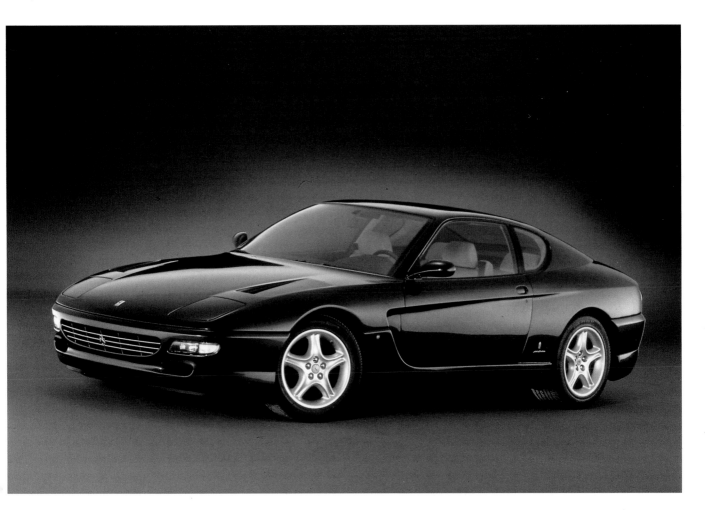

FERRARI 550 MARANELLO

Country of origin: Italy
Date: 1996
Engine: front-mounted quad ohc
65-degree V12, producing 357kW
(485bhp) at 7,000rpm
Transmission: 6-speed manual
Wheels driven: rear
Capacity: 5,474cc (334cu in)
Bore & stroke: 88 x 75mm (3.46 x 2.95in)
Performance: maximum speed
320km/h (199mph); 0–96.5km/h
(60mph) in 4.3 seconds
Dimensions: wheelbase 2.5m (8ft
2.43in); length 4.55m (14ft 11.13in);
width 1.935m (6ft 4.18in); height
1.277m (4ft 2.27in); track 1.623m (5ft
2.25in) front, 1.586m (5ft 2.44in) rear
Steering: ZF rack and pinion with
Servotronic speed-sensitive power
steering
Kerb weight: 1,690kg (3,726lb)
Fuel: 114l (25gal/30US gal)
Suspension: coil springs, anti-roll bars
Brakes: drilled discs front and rear
Compression ratio: 10.8 : 1

The 550 Maranello was an about-turn
for the Italian company; its latest
flagship supercar for the twenty-first
century has its engine at the front.

Ferrari set out to design a car that
offered exciting performance without
forgoing comfort; the quintessential
driving experience. In the 550, the
company has married state-of-the-art
technical advances with sophisticated

craftsmanship; combined speed and
acceleration with braking and
roadholding, soundproofing with
aerodynamic shape, and created a
supercar capable of completing the
Maranello test track faster than any
previous model.

The spiritual successor of the great
365 GTB/4, the Daytona, the 550
Maranello is the ultimate in a long
line of mid-engined supercars starting
with the Berlinetta Boxer of 1973.

The 550's bodywork is aluminium
over a tubular steel frame. Feran, an
advanced laminated sheet of steel
and aluminium, is laid between the
frame and the outer panels to enable
the two metals to be welded together.
Composites are used for the bumpers
and wheel-arch liners, and the body
itself was created by Pininfarina –
who else?

The 5.5-litre engine weighs 235kg
(518lb), with the cylinder case, the
head and oil sump in light alloy with
damp press-fitted aluminium cylinder
liners coated in Nikasil.

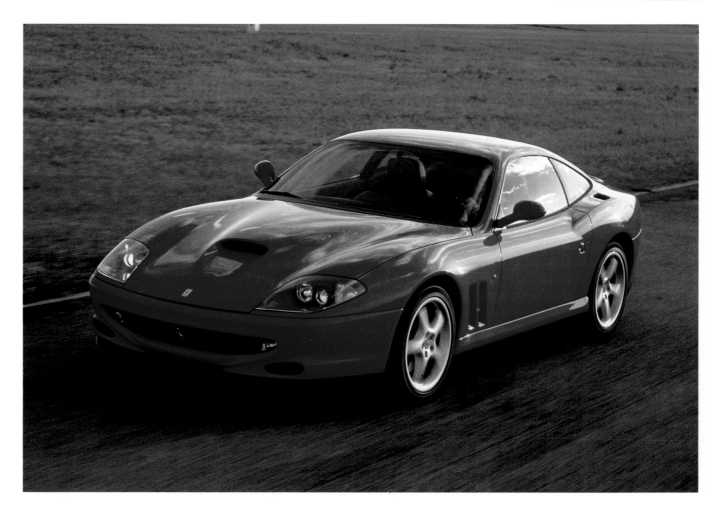

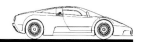

JAGUAR XK8

Country of origin: UK
Date: 1996
Engine: longitudinally front-mounted chain-driven dohc 90-degree V8 with 4 valves per cylinder, producing 216kW (290bhp) at 6,100rpm
Transmission: 5-speed automatic
Wheels driven: rear
Capacity: 3,996cc (243.9cu in)
Bore & stroke: 86 x 86mm (3.39 x 3.39in)
Performance: maximum speed 249.55km/h (155mph); 0–96.5km/h (60mph) in 6.4 seconds
Dimensions: wheelbase 2.588m (8ft 5.9in); length 4.76m (15ft 7.4in); width 2.015m (6ft 7.3in); height 1.296m (4ft 3in); track 1.504m (4ft 11.2in) front, 1.498m (4ft 11in) rear
Steering: rack and pinion
Kerb weight: 1,615kg (3,561lb)
Fuel: 75l (16.5gal/19.8US gal)
Suspension: coil springs and anti-roll bar front and rear
Brakes: ventilated discs front and rear
Compression ratio: 10.75 : 1

Looks, performance, grace and style were all commented upon by the press when Jaguar unveiled the long-awaited XK8. 'An outstandingly beautiful sports car which I am confident will take its place among the all-time greats in Jaguar's sports car history', said Nick Scheele, chairman and chief executive of Jaguar Cars, when the model was unveiled at the Geneva Motor show on 5 March 1996. The model was designed to succeed the XJ-S, Jaguar's best-selling car of all time with sales of approximately 112,000 units.

The styling of the XK8, which is available in both convertible and coupé versions, is contoured with the elegant and flowing lines that create a shape that is decidedly Jaguar. Its charismatic feline character is seen in its low stance at the front of the car accentuated by the traditional oval grille, the high waist-line and the muscular haunches that sweep over the rear wheels.

Jaguar's latest offering evokes the company's great sports legends of the past: the XK120, the C, D and E-Types, and more recently the XJ220.

At the heart of the XK8 is an all-new 4-litre AJ-V8 engine, delivering refined power for the company's newest generation of cars. This, Jaguar's very first V8 engine, endows the XK8 with both thrilling sports-car performance and exceptional refinement.

LOTUS ELISE

Country of origin: UK
Date: 1996
Engine: transversely mid-mounted dohc inline 4-cylinder with fuel injection, producing 88kW (118bhp) at 5,500rpm
Transmission: 5-speed automatic
Wheels driven: rear
Capacity: 1,796cc (109.6cu in)
Bore & stroke: 80 x 89.3mm (3.1 x 3.5in)
Performance: maximum speed 201km/h (124mph); 0–100km/h (62mph) in 5.9 seconds
Dimensions: wheelbase 2.3m (7ft 6.6in); length 3.726m (12ft 2.7in); width 1.701m (5ft 7in); height 1.202m (3ft 11.3in); track 1.44m (4ft 8.7in) front, 1.453m (4ft 9.2in) rear
Steering: rack and pinion
Kerb weight: 690kg (1,521lb)
Fuel: 40l (8.8gal/10.6US gal)
Suspension: double wishbones with coil springs front and rear
Brakes: ventilated discs front and rear
Compression ratio: 10.5 : 1

The Elise is a distinctive low-priced high-performance sports car of advanced race breeding, for which Lotus deserves recognition. The company has produced a terrifically innovative car, surely one destined to become a modern classic. Ignore the fact that Lotus was not in a position to produce a new engine in-house and so relied on the Rover K-series; what it has done is to take driving back to basics, and glove the phenomenal drive in a revolutionary aluminium chassis. The Elise is fast, light and fun to drive, with superb handling.

The enormously strong spaceframe chassis is fabricated from extruded anodised

aluminium, and bonded together with a special epoxy adhesive. A galvanised steel sub-frame carries the engine. The body comprises front and rear clamshell sections in composite materials.

The low body weight and resultant high power-to-weight ratio provide obvious benefits in performance, braking, handling and steering, as well as fuel consumption – an amazing 17.67km/l (49.9mpg) for extra urban driving – and emission levels. The attractive curvaceous shape of the Elise is also extremely aerodynamically effective; having been developed and finely honed in the wind tunnel, it includes chin and tail elements working with an underbody diffuser.

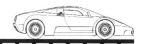

MERCEDES-BENZ SLK 230

Country of origin: Germany
Date: 1996
Engine: inline 4-cylinder with 4 valves per cylinder, producing 142kW (193bhp) at 5,300rpm
Transmission: 5-speed automatic
Wheels driven: rear
Capacity: 2,295cc (140cu in)
Bore & stroke: 90.9 x 88.4mm (3.58 x 3.48in)
Performance: maximum speed 230km/h (143mph); 0–96.5km/h (60mph) in 7.4 seconds
Dimensions: wheelbase 2.4m (7ft 10.5in); length 3.995m (13ft 1.3in); width 1.715m (5ft 7.5in); height 1.289m (4ft 2.7in); track 1.488m (4ft 10.6in) front, 1.485m (4ft 10.5in) rear
Kerb weight: 1,325kg (2,919lb)
Fuel: 53l (11.66gal/14US gal)
Suspension: dual wishbones with 2 triangular links front; multi-linked with anti-roll bars rear
Brakes: ABS
Compression ratio: 8.8 : 1

Launched during 1996, the SLK immediately piled up the orders, and today the waiting list is heading towards *four years*. And why not – it has Mercedes quality of build, oozes safety features such as acceleration skid control (ASC) braking and handles beautifully; furthermore, it's not bad-looking.

The SLK has a unique vario folding roof which, at the touch of a button, converts the roadster into a fixed-head coupé in a mere 25 seconds, with the boot lid moving backwards to accommodate it.

As for all new models, for the SLK Mercedes has made generous use of lightweight materials; inlet manifolds are high-specification plastic and cylinder heads are magnesium, which is also a material used in the car's structure. The road wheels are cast aluminium. At the heart of the SLK is the 2.3-litre Kompressor engine, a supercharged straight-four with variable camshafts, with the latest automatic engine management.

Mercedes is continuing the roadster tradition which began in the 1930s and was refined by the company in the 1950s with the 190SL; in creating the SLK, it has forsaken none of the standards of performance and quality that the motoring public has come to demand from Stuttgart.

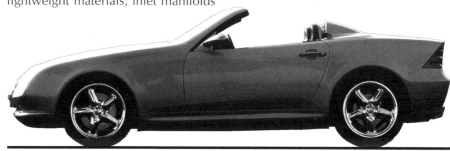

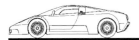

PORSCHE BOXSTER

Country of origin: Germany
Date: 1996
Engine: water-cooled quad ohc flat 6-cylinder, producing 150kW (204bhp) at 6,000rpm
Transmission: 5-speed manual
Wheels driven: rear
Capacity: 2,480cc (151.3cu in)
Bore & stroke: 85.5 x 72mm (3.37 x 2.83in)
Performance: maximum speed 240km/h (149mph); 0–96.5km/h (60mph) in 6.9 seconds
Dimensions: wheelbase 2.415m (7ft 11.1in); length 4.315m (14ft 1.9in); width 1.78m (5ft 10in); height 1.29m (4ft 2.8in); track 1.465m (4ft 9.7in) front, 1.524m (5ft) rear
Kerb weight: 1,250kg (2,756lb)
Fuel: 57l (12.5gal/15US gal)
Suspension: MacPherson struts front and rear; longitudinal and transverse control arms, spring struts and stump springs offset from the shock absorbers
Brakes: discs front and rear with ABS
Compression ratio: 11 : 1

The first all-new Porsche for 18 years was unveiled at the Paris motor show in October 1996. A two-seater mid-engined roadster, the Boxster captures the true spirit of Porsche's heritage of advanced design, performance and engineering excellence. The mid-engine provides ideal driving dynamics with the car's weight concentrated centrally so that the driver benefits from perfect balance and response. The engine is both smooth and efficient, featuring as it does dry-sump lubrication and a crossflow cooling system that ensures

constant temperature.

The Boxster has a monocoque body with body panels hot-galvanised on both sides, an all-steel bodyshell in the style of the classic early Porsche models such as the 1948 Porsche No 1 and the 550 Spyder of 1953. However, the Boxster's drag co-efficient is the best of its class at 0.31.

The roof system combines the optimum convertible qualities, with roof bars made of cast magnesium. A kinematic structure folds the roof like a letter Z before it disappears partly beneath the roof cover. The soft-top opening operation takes just 12 seconds.

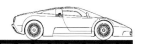

BMW Z3

Country of origin: Germany
Date: 1997
Engine: flat 6-cylinder with 4 valves per cylinder, producing 85kW (115bhp) at 5,500rpm
Transmission: 5-speed manual
Wheels driven: rear
Capacity: 1,795cc (109.5cu in)
Bore & stroke: 84 x 81mm (3.3 x 3.2in)
Performance: maximum speed 194km/h (120mph); 0–96.5km/h (60mph) in 10.5 seconds
Dimensions: wheelbase 2.446m (8ft 0.3in); length 4.025m (13ft 2.5in); width 1.692m (5ft 6.6in); height 1.288m (4ft 2.7in); track 1.411m (4ft 7.6in) front, 1.427m (4ft 8.2in) rear
Steering: power-assisted rack and pinion
Kerb weight: 1,160kg (2,558lb)
Suspension: single-joint spring strut axle with displaced camber front; independent semi-trailing arms, separate springs and dampers rear
Brakes: discs front and rear, with ABS
Compression ratio: 9.7 : 1

The Z3 is a two-seater sports car with a soft roof and was launched with the option of either a 1.8 or 1.9-litre 4-cylinder engine.Built at BMW's new plant in Spartanburg, South Carolina, the Z3 roadster is a successful blend of the absolutely modern and up-to-date yet redolent of nostalgia, with the attributes of BMW's roadsters of years gone by.

The familiar BMW kidney-shaped grille is fully integrated in the engine compartment lid, forming the typical roadster face of the marque. This is completed by round headlights and direction indicators under a common glass cover, the power bulge on the engine compartment lid, and the large air scoops in the integral front spoiler.

In profile the Z3 is distinctive, with its long bonnet and undulating waistline, steeply-raked windscreen, short rear section and compact front and rear overhangs, all of which contribute to creating traditional roadster proportions.

Maximum output is raised to 103kW (140bhp) with the larger 1.9-litre engine, the largest 4-cylinder that BMW makes; the top speed with the roof up is then increased to 205km/h (127mph). In November 1996, BMW announced the 2.8-litre 6-cylinder model, with acceleration of 0–100km/h (62mph) accomplished in a much-improved 7.1 seconds and a top speed of 218km/h (135mph).

PORSCHE 911 Carrera

Country of origin: Germany
Date: 1997
Engine: 6-cylinder quad ohc producing 221kW (300bhp) at 6,800 rpm
Transmission: 6 speed manual
Wheels driven: rear
Capacity: 3,387cc (207cu in)
Bore & stroke: 96 x 78mm (3.78 x 3.07in)
Performance: maximum speed 280km/h (174mph); 0–161km/h (100mph) in 11.5 secs
Dimensions: wheelbase 2.35m (7ft 8.5in); length 4.43m (14ft 6.4in); width 1.765m (5ft 9.5in); height 1.305m (4ft 3.4in); track with 457mm (18in) wheels 1.465m (4ft 9.7in) front, 1.48m (4ft 10.3in) rear
Steering: rack and pinion
Kerb weight: 1,320kg (2,910lb)
Fuel: 64l (14 gal/ 16.8US gal)
Suspension: front McPherson spring strut with independent suspension coil springs front and rear
Brakes: vented discs front and rear
Compression ratio: 11.3:1

Porsche first unveiled the 911 model in Paris in 1963. Now after 34 years of evolution the legend is reborn, as the most technically advanced, refined, capable and practical 911 ever.

It was designed from a clean sheet of paper by the Porsche design team, who have conjured an absolute knockout in performance as well as looks. They discarded the traditional roof line, unchanged since the first 911, and its sharp windscreen angle; introduced modified roof and doors, smoothed the flanks, flush-fitted the windows and reduced to a minimum both joints and seams, to create an aerodynamically improved harmony of curves overall.

Externally the car is unmistakenly 911, and it retains the essential character of its breeding with the 3.4-litre boxer engine still hanging out behind the rear wheels.

The venerable flat-six air-cooled engine has been usurped by a smaller yet more powerful multi-valved water-cooled version. A highly sophisticated engine management system is operated by digital motor electronics controlling the whole combustion process, while ten electronic control units are employed to report on the car's state of health to a central computer.

This latest generation of 911 is both wider and lighter, producing more internal space as well as an improved driving position.

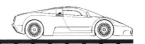

CHRONOLOGY 1940–1997

1940 Britain halts manufacture of cars for civilians as
production switches to military vehicles, and
imposes a night speed limit of 32km/h (20mph).

1941 The war years were characterised all over Europe by
– petrol rationing, night-time blackout and severe
1943 restrictions on the use of private cars.

1944 Standard buys out Triumph.
The Sports Car Club of America (SCCA) is formed.

1945 SS Cars Ltd is renamed Jaguar, and MG launches
the TC, as the auto industry races ahead to re-
launch pre-war models.

1946 The Triumph 1800 becomes the first British car to
have a column gearchange.
Renault launches its 4cv at the thirty-third Paris
motor show.
Austin buys Vanden Plas.

1947 Cisitalia launches the Pininfarina-designed 202
Gran Sport.
Henry Ford and Ettore Bugatti both die.
India bans car imports.
David Brown buys first Aston Martin, and then
Lagonda.

1948 Jaguar launches the world's fastest production car,
the XK120, at Britain's first post-war Motor Show.
The Issigonis-designed Morris Minor, the Jaguar Mk
V and the Land-Rover are also launched.

1949 The Citroën 2cv makes its début, as do the Rover P4
and Studebaker's Champion, with its wraparound
rear window. Other new models include the 203
from Peugeot and the Commodore from Hudson.

Above right: *Henry Ford sits atop his Quadricycle.
Ford was perhaps the most important figure of all
in the story of the automobile. He was born in
1863, the son of a father who was an immigrant
from Ireland and a mother of Dutch origin. His
first job was in Detroit with Flower Brothers, who
made machine tools. He moved on to the Dry
Dock Engine Company, and from there to a
company installing Westinghouse steam engines.
Ford married Clara Bryant in 1888, and set up a
small workshop where he spent his spare time
while working for the Detroit Edison Company.*

*When he was given permission by the town
council to use his first Quadricycle on public
roads, he left Edison and devoted his entire efforts
to the development of the motor car. Ford's
conception of the car was as transportation for the
masses; in order to achieve this, he cut costs all the
time, standardised whenever possible, and sold his
products at remarkably low prices. These social
and economic ideas were recorded in the books he
left behind on his death.*

Right: *a beautifully-restored 1940s MG TC*

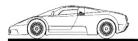

1950 Rover launches JET 1, the world's first jet-powered car.
Ford introduces the MacPherson strut, a combined oil-spring and damper.

1951 A C-Type Jaguar wins Le Mans and Appleyard wins the first of the revived RAC rallies in a Jaguar XK120.
Fangio wins the Swiss Grand Prix in Alfa's 159 racer.
Ferdinand Porsche dies on 30 January 1951.

1952 Dunlop designs the modern disc brake, a disc fixed to a rotating hub and clamped on each side by piston-operated pads.
The Healey 100 stops the show at Earl's Court.

1953 Dunlop manufactures the first tubeless tyres in Britain.
The World Sports Car Championship is inaugurated, with Ferrari as the first winners.
The Chevrolet Corvette becomes the first series-production car to have a fibreglass body
The AC Ace and Lotus Seven are revealed.
A Jaguar XK120C wins Le Mans.1

1954 Cadillac introduces power steering as standard.
The first car to have fuel injection as standard is the Mercedes gullwing 300SL.
Flashing indicators become legal on Britain's cars.

1955 A Jaguar D-Type wins the first of a trio of Le Mans victories.
The French Citroën DS19 model becomes the first production car to have front-wheel disc brakes, self-levelling suspension and detachable body panels.
The arrival of the MGA.

1956 The United States Auto Club (USAC) is formed to take over control of the four premier categories of racing in the USA.
Egypt closes the Suez Canal, leading to

international petrol restrictions.
Jaguar D-Types score a 1–2 at Le Mans.

1957 The last Mille Miglia is run.
A fire breaks out at Jaguar's Browns Lane factory, destroying the new XKSS models.
The first double white lines appear on Britain's roads.

1958 Lotus introduces the Elite, the first car with a unitary body and chassis construction in fibreglass.
The Austin-Healey Sprite and the Aston Martin DB4 make their débuts.

1959 The launch of Austin's Mini Seven and Morris Mini Minor.
Aston Martin wins Le Mans.
The Chevrolet Corvair becomes America's first rear-engined production car.

Above: *Ferdinand Porsche, seen here with his son Ferry and the No 1 Type 356 4-cylinder roadster; and below, a 1952 Mercedes-Benz 300SL*

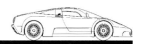

1960 The Marcos GT coupé goes into production with the first all-wooden unitary construction.
Armstrong Siddely ceases production.

1961 Jaguar launches the E-Type, the first 241km/h (150mph) production car.
Other new cars are the MG Midget, the Austin-Healey Sprite II and the Triumph TR4.
Graham Hill and Olivier Gendebien win at Le Mans driving a Ferrari 250TR.

1962 Volkswagen becomes the first European manufacturer to sell one million units of a single model in a year, the 'Beetle'.
Abingdon produces its first monocoque sports car, the 1800cc (110cu in) engined MGB.
Also new were the Lotus Elan and the Triumph Spitfire.

1963 The Wankel rotary engine enters production with NSU.
Mercedes launches the 230SL.
Jim Clark gains his first World Championship.
The Leyland Motor Corporation is formed.

1964 Cadillac introduces its climate control, the first fully automatic in-car air conditioning system.
A Mini Cooper S, *illustrated below*, gains a victory at Monte Carlo, driven by Paddy Hopkirk.
Chrysler Corporation buys into the Rootes Group.

1965 The VW 'Beetle' reaches its ten millionth example, and GM its ten millionth outside the USA.
Compulsory exhaust emission controls are introduced in California.
A new speed limit of 113km/h (70mph) is introduced in the UK.

1966 The first car to have 4-wheel drive combined with anti-lock brakes, the Jensen FF, is launched.
General Motors becomes the first car manufacturer to pass the one-hundred millionth mark.
The British Motor Corporation merges with Jaguar.

1967 Speed king Donald Campbell is killed.
The first Formula Ford race takes place at Brands Hatch.
Sweden switches from driving on the left to the right.
The breath test for alcohol is introduced in Britain.
The Leyland Motor Corporation takes over Rover.

1968 The last Austin-Healey is built, while the Reliant Scimitar GTE, the first proper sports estate, arrives.
Mercedes-Benz becomes the first European manufacturer to fit electronic fuel injection.
The Espada and the Morgan Plus Eight are launched.
British Leyland is formed, with a portfolio of 46 different marques.
The USA introduces stringent safety regulations on new cars, with worldwide repercussions.

1969 Ford USA offers an anti-lock braking system with rear-wheel sensors, and its GT40 wins Le Mans for the fourth consecutive time but only 10m (32ft 10in) ahead of a Porsche 908.
The Mini clocks up its two-millionth unit.

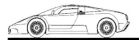

1970　The Datsun 240Z takes America by storm.
Mercedes reveals the Wankel-engined C111.
The Range Rover arrives, as do the Triumph Stag
and Marcos Mantis.

1971　Rolls-Royce goes bankrupt, and is nationalised.
A Porsche 917 short-tail wins Le Mans.
Maserati launches the V8 Bora, Jaguar the V12
E-Type and Lotus the Europa Twin-Cam.

1972　Matra makes it 1–2 at Le Mans.
British Leyland merges Rover with Triumph.
Graham Hill becomes the first driver to win Le
Mans, the Indianapolis 500 and the F1
championship.
David Brown sells Aston Martin to Company
Developments.

1973　General Motors offers the first safety airbag, in the USA.
The first acceleration booster is offered by BMW, on
the 2002 Turbo.
The MGB GT grows into a V8.
Bertone styles the first V8 road car for Ferrari, the
Dino 308 GT4.

1974　Aston Martin goes bankrupt, as does the British
Leyland Motor Corporation.
Lamborghini launches the Countach, Lotus the Elite
and Porsche the 911 Turbo.
Citroën merges with Peugeot.
The Lancia Stratos goes into production.

The Brinklin sports car makes its bow.

1975　Iso and Brinklin disappear.
De Tomaso snaps up Maserati.
Graham Hill dies.
The Triumph TR7 and Jaguar XJ-S are launched.

1976　Jensen halts car production.
The Audi 100 is the first mass-produced car to use a
5-cylinder engine.
Production of the Hillman Imp ends as Chrysler
kills off both the Hillman and the Humber marques.

1977　Earls Court holds its first Motorfair in what was not
a memorable year in the auto industry although
Concorde entered scheduled service and Elvis died.

1978　The Motor Show is held for the first time at the
NEC, Birmingham.
Chrysler sells its European operation to Peugeot,
which thus becomes Europe's largest car company.
The British Government promises De Lorean £52m
to build his car in Northern Ireland.
Lamborghini's Countach and Ferrari's 512 BB fail to
impress the motoring press.

1979　Ford buys a 20 per cent share of Mazda.
Volkswagen launches the Golf.
Renault buys 46 per cent of American Motors.
The UK buys 58 per cent of its cars from abroad.

Below: *a British-registered Datsun 240Z*

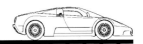

1980 MG closes its factory, the last Abingdon car being an MG BGT.
The 4-wheel drive Audi Quattro turbocharges onto the scene, as well as TVR's first new car since it was founded, the Tasmin.

1981 Hello to the De Lorean; the DMC-2, first unveiled in 1976, hits the show rooms.
Other new cars this year are the Porsche 944 and the Maserati Biturbo.
Aston Martin is sold again, the renamed business being Aston Martin Lagonda.

1982 Farewell to Lotus founder Colin Chapman and to Gilles Villeneuve; the latter dies while practising for the Belgian Grand Prix.
Goodbye to De Lorean; the company is liquidated.

1983 Seat belts are made compulsory in the UK.
Honda and Williams team up in Formula One but Ford pulls out of competition.
The Dutch motorway police refuse to swap their Porsches for BMW 323s.
Aston Martin is sold again.

1984 Ferrari launches the Testarossa and the GTO.
AC is sold.
The first all-turbo F1 race takes place at Monza.
Jaguar Cars is privatised.

1985 Renault rings up losses in excess of £1billion.
Farewells to Sir William Lyons, the Porsche 924 and the Citroën Dyane.
Volkswagen takes control of Seat from Fiat.
Chrysler buys into Maserati.

Above right: *a young Enzo Ferrari in 1920, taking part in his second Targa Florio; and* **below,** *a 1985 Audi Sport Quattro showers onlookers with dust*

1986 General Motors takes a controlling interest in Lotus.
Sports car technology reaches new heights with the limited-production Porsche 959.
Wheel clamping comes to London, together with unleaded petrol.
The car celebrates its centenary.
The five-millionth Mini is produced.

1987 Ford takes 75 per cent of Aston Martin and all of AC Cars.
Ferrari celebrates 40 years of sports car production by launching the F40, a 322km/h (200mph) souvenir of the screamers of the muscle car era.
A Bugatti Royale goes under the hammer at £5.5 million.
A German journalist clocks up 317km/h (197mph) on an Autobahn at the wheel of a Porsche 959.
Chrysler buys AMC and Lamborghini.

1988 Jaguar shows the super-expensive XJ220 as a concept car, and celebrates with its first Le Mans victory since 1957.
BMW launches its first-ever estate car, the 3-series Touring.
Sir Alec Issigonis, Donald Healey and, perhaps the greatest of all motoring legends, Enzo Ferrari, are mourned.

1989 Ford takes over Jaguar.
Honda buys into Rover.
A plethora of new sports models are announced.
A Porsche 911 is clocked at 347.5km/h (216mph) on the Autobahn.

Above: *Mazda gave us the small V6 at the heart of the MX-3 in 1991*

1990 AC Cars is liquidated by Ford.
Reliant also bows out.
The Mini-Cooper reappears, and the Citroën 2cv is laid to rest.
Jaguars score 1–2 at Le Mans.

1991 Bugatti's EB110 is launched.
At last the M40 London to Birmingham motorway is completed.
Mazda's MX-3 has the world's smallest V6 at 1.8 litres (110cu in).
The last of the Trabants falls off the production line.

1992 Ginetta goes bankrupt but later reappears.
Lotus ditches the Elan.
Ferrari employees are put on short-time working.

1993 Bugatti buys Lotus.
The DB7 heralds a new chapter in the Aston Martin story.
Ferruccio Lamborghini dies, also ex-World Champion James Hunt.
After 32 years of faithful service, the Renault 4 bows out.

1994 BMW buys Rover.
The Ford Probe becomes the first US-built Ford to be marketed in the UK for 70 years. Ford also takes the remaining 25% of Aston Martin.

1995 McLaren wins Le Mans.
Bugatti Automobile SpA is declared bankrupt.
MG is reborn, with the launch of the MGF.

Below: *the MG marque returned with the MGF in 1995*

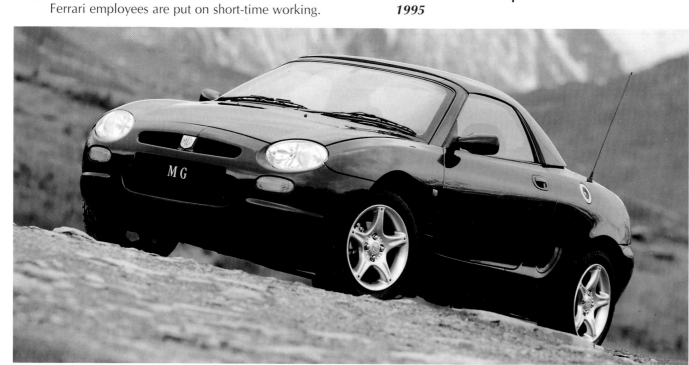

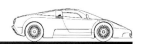

1996 A whole new clutch of sports cars are launched by BMW, Jaguar, Mercedes, Caterham, and Ferrari; all mark the centenary of the registration of the Daimler Motor Company, the first UK-registered car company.

1997 Porsche builds its one-millionth car.
GM launches the new-generation Corvette, and the twenty-first century is in sight.
Porsche, which has taken more victories there than any other manufacturer, chalks up another win at the sixty-fifth running of Le Mans.

Above: *Ferrari celebrates, with its aptly-designated F50*

Richard Noble's *Thrust SSC* team establishes a new land speed record when driver Andy Green breaks the sound barrier to establish a speed of 1,226km/h (762mph). A century earlier, the land speed record stood at 63.14km/h (39.24mph).

Below: *the 1998 model year Chevrolet Corvette is the fifth generation of the model*

INDEX OF MODELS

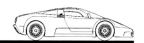

GENERAL INDEX

CHEVROLET CORVETTE

Country of origin: USA
Date: 1997
Engine: front-mounted ohv 90-degree V8 with 2 valves per cylinder, producing 251kW (339bhp) at 5,400rpm
Transmission: 4-speed automatic
Wheels driven: rear
Capacity: 5,660cc (345cu in)
Bore & stroke: 99 x 92mm (3.9 x 3.6in)
Performance: maximum speed 275.1km/h (171mph); 0–96.5km/h (60mph) in 5.7 seconds
Dimensions: wheelbase 2.656m (8ft 8.6in); length 4.565m (14ft 11.7in); width 2.01m (6ft 7.1in); height 1.211m (3ft 11.7in); track 1.575m (5ft 2in) front and rear
Steering: power-assisted rack and pinion
Kerb weight: 1,471kg (3,240lb)
Fuel: 72l (15.9gal/19.1US gal)
Suspension: double wishbones, leaf springs, dampers and anti-roll bars front and rear
Brakes: ventilated discs front, discs rear
Compression ratio: 10 : 1

The very latest Corvette is the fifth generation of the longest-lived sports car in the world. Launched in 1953, it exuded style even if the original V8 performance was lacking. It was a fibreglass-bodied two-seater that went on to become America's best-selling sports car ever, with sales in excess of 1.1 million. As such, it is the ideal model with which to end this century of the sports car.

The new Corvette is better-looking than ever, undoubtedly has supercar performance and comes to the showroom at a price that leaves it without a competitor. Re-engineered, restyled and repackaged with a Cd of 0.29 and a fuel consumption of 5.06km/l (14.3mpg) EU urban, it offers more cabin space and cleverly-laid out instrumentation. After a production run of about 60 million, GM's small-block V8 is stood down in favour of a new aluminium alloy V8 that makes its début in the Corvette. Though it does stick to the old pushrod design, the manifold is made of composite plastic and the intake ports are all straight and of equal length. In order to achieve a better weight distribution, the gearbox has been moved from directly behind the engine to a positioon over the rear axle, producing a near-perfect 51:49. Although the ride still leaves room for improvement, this is one Corvette that has definitely come of age and is ready for the twenty-first century.

ACKNOWLEDGMENTS

Superlaunch Ltd have pleasure in thanking the many manufacturers who have generously contributed information and illustrations, and without whose support this book would not have been possible.

We hope that all our readers everywhere will be inspired by this book to feel gratitude for all those endeavours of the manufacturers, designers and creators of the marques that are no longer with us at the close of this century, for the legacy of the tangible results of their skills and imagination which continue to give us enjoyment today.

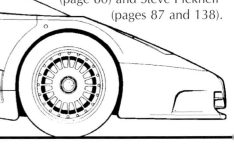